SOCIALISM

Utopian and Scientific

by Frederick Engels

WITH THE ESSAY ON "THE MARK"

Translated by Edward Aveling

INTERNATIONAL PUBLISHERS
New York

This printing 1994

ISBN 0-7178-0191-8

INTERNATIONAL PUBLISHERS CO., INC.

PRINTED IN THE U.S.A.

CONTENTS

SOCIALISM
UTOPIAN AND SCIENTIFIC

INTRODUCTION

THE PRESENT little book is, originally, a part of a larger whole. About 1875, Dr. E. Dühring, *privatdocent* at Berlin University, suddenly and rather clamorously announced his conversion to socialism, and presented the German public not only with an elaborate socialist theory, but also with a complete practical plan for the reorganisation of society. As a matter of course, he fell foul of his predecessors; above all, he honoured Marx by pouring out upon him the full vials of his wrath.

This took place about the time when the two sections of the Socialist Party in Germany—Eisenachers and Lassalleans—had just effected their fusion, and thus obtained not only an immense increase of strength, but, what was more, the faculty of employing the whole of this strength against the common enemy. The Socialist Party in Germany was fast becoming a power. But to make it a power, the first condition was that the newly-conquered unity should not be imperilled. And Dr. Dühring openly proceeded to form around himself a sect, the nucleus of a future separate party. It thus became necessary to take up the gauntlet thrown down to us, and to fight out the struggle whether we liked it or not.

This, however, though it might not be an over-difficult, was evidently a long-winded, business. As is well known, we Germans are of a terribly ponderous *Gründlichkeit*, radical profundity or profound radicality, whatever you may like to call it. Whenever any one of us expounds what he considers a new doctrine, he has first to elaborate it into an all-comprising system. He has to prove that both the first principles of logic and the fundamental laws of the universe had existed from all eternity for no other purpose than to ultimately lead to this newly-discovered, crowning theory. And Dr. Dühring, in this respect, was quite up to the national mark. Nothing less than a complete *System of Philosophy*, mental, moral, natural and

7

historical; a complete *System of Political Economy and Socialism;* and, finally, a *Critical History of Political Economy* —three big volumes in octavo, heavy extrinsically and intrinsically, three army corps of arguments mobilised against all previous philosophers and economists in general, and against Marx in particular—in fact, an attempt at a complete "revolution in science"—these were what I should have to tackle. I had to treat of all and every possible subject from the concepts of time and space to bimetallism; from the eternity of matter and motion to the perishable nature of moral ideas; from Darwin's natural selection to the education of youth in a future society. Anyhow, the systematic comprehensiveness of my opponent gave me the opportunity of developing, in opposition to him, and in a more connected form than had previously been done, the views held by Marx and myself on this great variety of subjects. And that was the principal reason which made me undertake this otherwise ungrateful task.

My reply was first published in a series of articles in the Leipzig *Vorwärts,* the chief organ of the Socialist Party, and later on as a book: *Herrn Eugen Dühring's Umwälzung der Wissenschaft,** a second edition of which appeared in Zürich, 1886.

At the request of my friend, Paul Lafargue, now representative of Lille in the French Chamber of Deputies, I arranged three chapters of this book as a pamphlet, which he translated and published in 1880, under the title: *Socialisme utopique et Socialisme scientifique.* From this French text a Polish and a Spanish edition were prepared. In 1883 our German friends brought out the pamphlet in the original language. Italian, Russian, Danish, Dutch and Rumanian translations, based upon the German text, have since been published. Thus, with the present English edition, this little book circulates in ten languages. I am not aware that any other socialist work, not even our *Communist Manifesto* of 1848 or Marx's *Capital,* has been so often translated. In Germany it has had four editions of about 20,000 copies in all.

The appendix, *The Mark,* was written with the intention of

* *Herr Eugen Dühring's Revolution in Science* (International Publishers).—*Ed.*

spreading among the German Socialist Party some elementary knowledge of the history and development of landed property in Germany. This seemed all the more necessary at a time when the assimilation by that party of the working people of the towns was in a fair way of completion, and when the agricultural labourers and peasants had to be taken in hand. This appendix has been included in the translation, as the original forms of tenure of land common to all Teutonic tribes, and the history of their decay, are even less known in England than in Germany. I have left the text as it stands in the original, without alluding to the hypothesis recently started by Maxim Kovalevsky, according to which the partition of the arable and meadow lands among the members of the mark was preceded by their being cultivated for joint account by a large patriarchal family community embracing several generations (as exemplified by the still existing South Slavonian Zadruga), and that the partition, later on, took place when the community had increased, so as to become too unwieldy for joint-account management. Kovalevsky is probably quite right, but the matter is still *sub judice.*

The economic terms used in this work, as far as they are new, agree with those used in the English edition of Marx's *Capital.* We call "production of commodities" that economic phase where articles are produced not only for the use of the producers, but also for purposes of exchange; that is, *as commodities,* not as use values. This phase extends from the first beginnings of production for exchange down to our present time; it attains its full development under capitalist production only, that is, under conditions where the capitalist, the owner of the means of production, employs, for wages, labourers, people deprived of all means of production except their own labour power, and pockets the excess of the selling price of the products over his outlay. We divide the history of industrial production since the Middle Ages into three periods: 1) handicraft, small master craftsmen with a few journeymen and apprentices, where each labourer produces the complete article; 2) manufacture, where greater numbers of workmen, grouped in one large establishment, produce the complete article on the principle of division of labour, each workman performing only one partial operation, so that the product is complete only after having passed successively through the hands of all; 3) modern industry, where the product is produced by machinery driven by power, and where the work of the labourer is limited to superintending and correcting the performances of the mechanical agent.

I am perfectly aware that the contents of this work will meet with objection from a considerable portion of the British public. But if we Continentals had taken the slightest notice of the prejudices of British "respectability," we should be even worse off than we are. This book defends what we call "historical materialism," and the word materialism grates upon the ears of the immense majority of British readers. "Agnosticism" might be tolerated, but materialism is utterly inadmissible.

And yet the original home of all modern materialism, from the seventeenth century onwards, is England.

Materialism is the natural-born son of Great Britain. Already the British schoolman, Duns Scotus, asked, "whether it was impossible for matter to think?"

In order to effect this miracle, he took refuge in God's omnipotence, i.e., he made theology preach materialism. Moreover, he was a nominalist. Nominalism, the first form of materialism, is chiefly found among the English schoolmen.

The real progenitor of English materialism is Bacon. To him natural philosophy is the only true philosophy, and physics based upon the experience of the senses is the chiefest part of natural philosophy. Anaxagoras and his homœomeriæ, Democritus and his atoms, he often quotes as his authorities. According to him the senses are infallible and the source of all knowledge. All science is based on experience, and consists in subjecting the data furnished by the senses to a rational method of investigation. Induction, analysis, comparison, observation, experiment, are the principal forms of such a rational method. Among the qualities inherent in matter, motion is the first and foremost, not only in the form of mechanical and mathematical motion, but chiefly in the form of an impulse, a vital spirit, a tension—or a "qual," to use a term of Jacob Böhme's *—of matter.

* "Qual" is a philosophical play upon words. Qual literally means torture, a pain which drives to action of some kind; at the same time the mystic Böhme puts into the German word something of the meaning of

In Bacon, its first creator, materialism still occludes within itself the germs of a many-sided development. On the one hand, matter, surrounded by a sensuous, poetic glamour, seems to attract man's whole entity by winning smiles. On the other, the aphoristically formulated doctrine pullulates with inconsistencies imported from theology.

In its further evolution, materialism becomes one-sided. Hobbes is the man who systematises Baconian materialism. Knowledge based upon the senses loses its poetic blossom, it passes into the abstract experience of the mathematician; geometry is proclaimed as the queen of sciences. Materialism takes to misanthropy. If it is to overcome its opponent, misanthropic, fleshless spiritualism, and that on the latter's own ground, materialism has to chastise its own flesh and turn ascetic. Thus, from a sensual, it passes into an intellectual entity; but thus, too, it evolves all the consistency, regardless of consequences, characteristic of the intellect.

Hobbes, as Bacon's continuator, argues thus: If all human knowledge is furnished by the senses, then our concepts and ideas are but the phantoms, divested of their sensual forms, of the real world. Philosophy can but give names to these phantoms. One name may be applied to more than one of them. There may even be names of names. It would imply a contradiction if, on the one hand, we maintained that all ideas had their origin in the world of sensation, and, on the other, that a word was more than a word; that besides the beings known to us by our senses, beings which are one and all individuals, there existed also beings of a general, not individual, nature. An unbodily substance is the same absurdity as an unbodily body. Body, being, substance, are but different terms for the same reality. *It is impossible to separate thought from matter that thinks.* This matter is the substratum of all changes going on in the world. The word infinite is meaningless, unless it states that our mind is capable of performing an endless process of addition. Only material things being perceptible to us, we cannot know anything about the existence of God. My own existence alone is certain. Every human passion is a mechanical movement which has a beginning and an end. The objects of impulse are what we call good. Man is subject to the same laws as nature. Power and freedom are identical.

Hobbes had systematised Bacon, without, however, furnishing a proof for Bacon's fundamental principle, the origin of all human

the Latin *qualitas;* his "qual" was the activating principle arising from, and promoting in its turn, the spontaneous development of the thing, relation, or person subject to it, in contradistinction to a pain inflicted from without.

knowledge from the world of sensation. It was Locke who, in his *Essay on the Human Understanding,* supplied this proof.

Hobbes had shattered the theistic prejudices of Baconian materialism; Collins, Dodwall, Coward, Hartley, Priestley similarly shattered the last theological bars that still hemmed in Locke's sensationalism. At all events, for practical materialists, theism is but an easy-going way of getting rid of religion.*

Thus Karl Marx wrote about the British origin of modern materialism. If Englishmen nowadays do not exactly relish the compliment he paid their ancestors, more's the pity. It is none the less undeniable that Bacon, Hobbes and Locke are the fathers of that brilliant school of French materialists which made the eighteenth century, in spite of all battles on land and sea won over Frenchmen by Germans and Englishmen, a preeminently French century, even before that crowning French Revolution, the results of which we outsiders, in England as well as in Germany, are still trying to acclimatise.

There is no denying it. About the middle of this century, what struck every cultivated foreigner who set up his residence in England was what he was then bound to consider the religious bigotry and stupidity of the English respectable middle class. We, at that time, were all materialists, or, at least, very advanced freethinkers, and to us it appeared inconceivable that almost all educated people in England should believe in all sorts of impossible miracles and that even geologists like Buckland and Mantell should contort the facts of their science so as not to clash too much with the myths of the book of Genesis; while, in order to find people who dared to use their own intellectual faculties with regard to religious matters, you had to go amongst the uneducated, the "great unwashed," as they were then called, the working people, especially the Owenite socialists.

But England has been "civilised" since then. The exhibition of 1851 sounded the knell of English insular exclusiveness. England became gradually internationalised, in diet, in manners, in ideas; so much so that I begin to wish that some English manners and customs had made as much headway on the Continent as other Continental habits have made here. Anyhow,

* Marx and Engels, *Die Heilige Familie,* Frankfurt a. M., 1845, pp. 201-04.

the introduction and spread of salad oil (before 1851 known only to the aristocracy) has been accompanied by a fatal spread of continental scepticism in matters religious, and it has come to this, that agnosticism, though not yet considered "the thing" quite as much as the Church of England, is yet very nearly on a par, as far as respectability goes, with Baptism, and decidedly ranks above the Salvation Army. And I cannot help believing that under these circumstances it will be consoling to many who sincerely regret and condemn this progress of infidelity, to learn that these "new-fangled notions" are not of foreign origin, are not "made in Germany," like so many other articles of daily use, but are undoubtedly Old English, and that their British originators two hundred years ago went a good deal further than their descendants now dare to venture.

What, indeed, is agnosticism, but, to use an expressive Lancashire term, "shamefaced" materialism? The agnostic's conception of nature is materialistic throughout. The entire natural world is governed by law, and absolutely excludes the intervention of action from without. But, he adds, we have no means either of ascertaining or of disproving the existence of some supreme being beyond the known universe. Now, this might hold good at the time when Laplace, to Napoleon's question, why in the great astronomer's *Mécanique céleste* the Creator was not even mentioned, proudly replied: *"Je n'avais pas besoin de cette hypothèse."* But nowadays, in our evolutionary conception of the universe, there is absolutely no room for either a creator or a ruler; and to talk of a supreme being shut out from the whole existing world implies a contradiction in terms, and as it seems to me, a gratuitous insult to the feelings of religious people.

Again, our agnostic admits that all our knowledge is based upon the information imparted to us by our senses. But, he adds, how do we know that our senses give us correct representations of the objects we perceive through them? And he proceeds to inform us that, whenever he speaks of objects or their qualities, he does in reality not mean these objects and qualities, of which he cannot know anything for certain, but merely the impressions which they have produced on his senses. Now, this line of reasoning seems undoubtedly hard to beat by mere argumentation. But before there was argumentation, there was action. *Im Anfang war die That.* And human action had solved the difficulty long before human ingenuity invented it. The proof of the pudding is in the eating. From the moment we turn to our own use these objects, according to the qualities we perceive in them, we put to an infallible test the correctness or otherwise of our sense perceptions. If these perceptions have been wrong, then our estimate of the use to which an object can be turned must also be wrong, and our attempt must fail. But if we succeed in accomplishing our aim, if we find that the object does agree with our idea of it, and does answer the purpose we intended it for, then that is positive proof that our perceptions of it and of its qualities, *so far,* agree with reality outside ourselves. And whenever we find ourselves face to face with a failure, then we generally are not long in making out the cause that made us fail; we find that the perception upon which we acted was either incomplete and superficial, or combined with the result of other perceptions in a way not warranted by them—what we call defective reasoning. So long as we take care to train and to use our senses properly, and to keep our action within the limits prescribed by perceptions properly made and properly used, so long we shall find that the result of our action proves the conformity of our perceptions with the objective nature of the things perceived. Not in one single instance, so far, have we been led to the conclusion that our sense perceptions, scientifically controlled, induce in our minds ideas respecting the outer world that are, by their very nature, at variance with reality, or that there is an inherent incompatibility between the outer world and our sense perceptions of it.

But then come the Neo-Kantian agnostics and say: We may correctly perceive the qualities of a thing, but we cannot by any sensible or mental process grasp the thing in itself. This "thing in itself" is beyond our ken. To this Hegel, long since, has replied: If you know all the qualities of a thing, you know the thing itself; nothing remains but the fact that the said thing exists without us; and when your senses have taught you that fact, you have grasped the last remnant of the thing in itself, Kant's celebrated unknowable *Ding an sich.* To which it may be added, that in Kant's time our knowledge of natural objects was indeed so fragmentary that he might well suspect, behind the little we knew about each of them, a mysterious "thing in itself." But one after another these ungraspable things have been grasped, analysed, and, what is more, *reproduced* by the giant progress of science; and what we can produce, we certainly cannot consider as unknowable. To the chemistry of the first half of this century organic substances were such mysterious objects; now we learn to build them up one after another from their chemical elements without the aid of organic processes. Modern chemists declare that as soon as the chemical constitution of no matter what body is known, it can be built up from its elements. We are still far from knowing the constitution of the highest organic substances, the albuminous bodies; but there is no reason why we should not, if only after centuries, arrive at that knowledge and, armed with it, produce artificial albumen. But if we arrive at that, we shall at the same time have produced organic life, for life, from its lowest to its highest forms, is but the normal mode of existence of albuminous bodies.

As soon, however, as our agnostic has made these formal mental reservations, he talks and acts as the rank materialist he at bottom is. He may say that, as far as *we* know, matter and motion, or as it is now called, energy, can neither be created nor destroyed, but that we have no proof of their not having been created at some time or other. But if you try to use this admission against him in any particular case, he will quickly put you out of court. If he admits the possibility of spiritualism *in abstracto,* he will have none of it *in concreto.* As far as we know and can know, he will tell you there is no Creator and no Ruler of the universe; as far as we are concerned, matter and energy can neither be created nor annihilated; for us, mind is a mode of energy, a function of the brain; all we know is that the material world is governed by immutable laws, and so forth. Thus, as far as he is a scientific man, as far as he *knows* anything, he is a materialist; outside his science, in spheres about which he knows nothing, he translates his ignorance into Greek and calls it agnosticism.

At all events, one thing seems clear: even if I was an agnostic, it is evident that I could not describe the conception of history sketched out in this little book, as "historical agnosticism." Religious people would laugh at me, agnostics would indignantly ask, was I going to make fun of them? And thus I hope even British respectability will not be overshocked if I use, in English, as well as in so many other languages the term "historical materialism," to designate that view of the course of history, which seeks the ultimate cause and the great moving power of all important historic events in the economic development of society, in the changes in the modes of production and exchange, in the consequent division of society into distinct classes, and in the struggles of these classes against one another.

This indulgence will perhaps be accorded to me all the sooner if I show that historical materialism may be of advantage even to British respectability. I have mentioned the fact that, about forty or fifty years ago, any cultivated foreigner settling in England was struck by what he was then bound to consider the religious bigotry and stupidity of the English respectable middle class. I am now going to prove that the respectable English middle class of that time was not quite as stupid as it looked to the intelligent foreigner. Its religious leanings can be explained.

When Europe emerged from the Middle Ages, the rising middle class of the towns constituted its revolutionary element. It had conquered a recognised position within mediæval feudal organisation, but this position, also, had become too narrow for its expansive power. The development of the middle class, the *bourgeoisie,* became incompatible with the maintenance of the feudal system; the feudal system, therefore, had to fall.

But the great international centre of feudalism was the Roman Catholic Church. It united the whole of feudalised Western Europe, in spite of all internal wars, into one grand political system, opposed as much to the schismatic Greek as to the Mohammedan countries. It surrounded feudal institutions with the halo of divine consecration. It had organised its own hierarchy on the feudal model, and, lastly, it was itself by far the most powerful feudal lord, holding, as it did, fully one-third of the soil of the Catholic world. Before profane feudalism could be successfully attacked in each country and in detail, this, its sacred central organisation, had to be destroyed.

Moreover, parallel with the rise of the middle class went on the great revival of science; astronomy, mechanics, physics, anatomy, physiology, were again cultivated. And the bourgeoisie, for the development of its industrial production, required a science which ascertained the physical properties of natural objects and the modes of action of the forces of nature. Now up to then science had but been the humble handmaid of the Church, had not been allowed to overstep the limits set by faith, and for that reason had been no science at all. Science rebelled against the Church; the bourgeoisie could not do without science, and, therefore, had to join in the rebellion.

The above, though touching but two of the points where the rising middle class was bound to come into collision with the established religion, will be sufficient to show, first, that the class most directly interested in the struggle against the pretensions of the Roman Church was the bourgeoisie; and second, that every struggle against feudalism, at that time, had to take on a religious disguise, had to be directed against the Church in the first instance. But if the universities and the traders of the cities started the cry, it was sure to find, and did find, a strong echo in the masses of the country people, the peasants, who everywhere had to struggle for their very existence with their feudal lords, spiritual and temporal.

The long fight of the bourgeoisie against feudalism culminated in three great decisive battles.

The first was what is called the Protestant Reformation in Germany. The war-cry raised against the Church by Luther was responded to by two insurrections of a political nature: first, that of the lower nobility under Franz von Sickingen (1523), then the great Peasants' War, 1525. Both were defeated, chiefly in consequence of the indecision of the parties most interested, the burghers of the towns—an indecision into the causes of which we cannot here enter. From that moment the struggle degenerated into a fight between the local princes and the central power, and ended by blotting out Germany, for two hundred years, from the politically active nations of Europe. The Lutheran reformation produced a new creed indeed, a religion adapted to absolute monarchy. No sooner were the peasants of Northeast Germany converted to Lutheranism than they were from freemen reduced to serfs.

But where Luther failed, Calvin won the day. Calvin's creed was one fit for the boldest of the bourgeoisie of his time. His predestination doctrine was the religious expression of the fact that in the commercial world of competition success or failure does not depend upon a man's activity or cleverness, but upon circumstances uncontrollable by him. It is not of him that willeth or of him that runneth, but of the mercy of unknown superior economic powers; and this was especially true at a period of economic revolution, when all old commercial routes and centres were replaced by new ones, when India and America were opened to the world, and when even the most sacred economic articles of faith—the value of gold and silver—began to totter and to break down. Calvin's church constitution was thoroughly democratic and republican; and where the kingdom of God was republicanised, could the kingdoms of this world remain subject to monarchs, bishops and lords? While German Lutheranism became a willing tool in the hands of princes, Calvinism founded a republic in Holland and active republican parties in England, and, above all, Scotland.

In Calvinism, the second great bourgeois upheaval found its doctrine ready cut and dried. This upheaval took place in England. The middle class of the towns brought it on, and the yeomanry of the country districts fought it out. Curiously enough, in all the three great bourgeois risings, the peasantry furnishes the army that has to do the fighting; and the peasantry is just the class that, the victory once gained, is most surely ruined by the economic consequences of that victory. A hundred years after Cromwell, the yeomanry of England had almost disappeared. Anyhow, had it not been for that yeomanry and for the *plebeian* element in the towns, the bourgeoisie alone would never have fought the matter out to the bitter end, and would never have brought Charles I to the scaffold. In order to secure even those conquests of the bourgeoisie that were ripe for gathering at the time, the revolution had to be carried considerably further—exactly as in 1793 in France and 1848 in Germany. This seems, in fact, to be one of the laws of evolution of bourgeois society.

Well, upon this excess of revolutionary activity there necessarily followed the inevitable reaction which in its turn went beyond the point where it might have maintained itself. After a series of oscillations, the new centre of gravity was at last attained and became a new starting point. The grand period of English history, known to respectability under the name of "the Great Rebellion," and the struggles succeeding it, were brought to a close by the comparatively puny event entitled by Liberal historians, "the Glorious Revolution."

The new starting point was a compromise between the rising middle class and the ex-feudal landowners. The latter, though called, as now, the aristocracy, had been long since on the way which led them to become what Louis Philippe in France became at a much later period, "the first bourgeois of the kingdom." Fortunately for England, the old feudal barons had killed one another during the Wars of the Roses. Their successors, though mostly scions of the old families, had been so much out of the direct line of descent that they constituted quite a new body, with habits and tendencies far more bourgeois than feudal. They fully understood the value of money, and at once began to increase their rents by turning hundreds of small farmers out and replacing them by sheep. Henry VIII, while squandering the Church lands, created fresh bourgeois landlords by wholesale; the innumerable confiscations of estates, regranted to absolute or relative upstarts, and continued during the whole of the seventeenth century, had the same result. Consequently, ever since Henry VII, the English "aristocracy," far from counteracting the development of industrial production, had, on the contrary, sought to indirectly profit thereby; and there had always been a section of the great landowners willing, from economical or political reasons, to co-operate with the leading men of the financial and industrial bourgeoisie. The compromise of 1689 was, therefore, easily accomplished. The political spoils of "pelf and place" were left to the great landowning families, provided the economic interests of the financial, manufacturing and commercial middle class were sufficiently attended to. And these economic interests were at that time powerful enough to determine the general policy of the nation. There might be squabbles about matters of detail, but, on the whole, the aristocratic oligarchy knew too well that its own economic prosperity was irretrievably bound up with that of the industrial and commercial middle class.

From that time, the bourgeoisie was a humble, but still a recognised component of the ruling classes of England. With the rest of them, it had a common interest in keeping in subjection the great working mass of the nation. The merchant or manufacturer himself stood in the position of master, or, as it was until lately called, of "natural superior" to his clerks, his workpeople, his domestic servants. His interest was to get as much and as good work out of them as he could; for this end they had to be trained to proper submission. He was himself religious; his religion had supplied the standard under which he had fought the king and the lords; he was not long in discovering the opportunities this same religion offered him for working upon the minds of his natural inferiors, and making them submissive to the behests of the masters it had pleased God to place over them. In short, the English bourgeoisie now had to take a part in keeping down the "lower orders," the great producing mass of the nation, and one of the means employed for that purpose was the influence of religion.

There was another fact that contributed to strengthen the religious leanings of the bourgeoisie. That was the rise of materialism in England. This new doctrine not only shocked the pious feelings of the middle class; it announced itself as a philosophy only fit for scholars and cultivated men of the world, in contrast to religion which was good enough for the uneducated masses, including the bourgeoisie. With Hobbes it stepped on the stage as a defender of royal prerogative and omnipotence; it called upon absolute monarchy to keep down that *puer robustus sed malitiosus*, to wit, the people. Similarly, with the successors of Hobbes, with Bolingbroke, Shaftesbury, etc., the new deistic form of materialism remained an aristocratic, esoteric doctrine, and, therefore, hateful to the middle class both for its religious heresy and for its anti-bourgeois political connections. Accordingly, in opposition to the materialism and deism of the aristocracy, those Protestant sects which had furnished the flag and the fighting contingent against the Stuarts, continued to furnish the main strength of the progressive middle class, and form even today the backbone of "the Great Liberal Party."

In the meantime materialism passed from England to France, where it met and coalesced with another materialistic school of philosophers, a branch of Cartesianism. In France, too, it remained at first an exclusively aristocratic doctrine. But soon its revolutionary character asserted itself. The French materialists did not limit their criticism to matters of religious belief; they extended it to whatever scientific tradition or political institution they met with; and to prove the claim of their doctrine to universal application, they took the shortest cut, and boldly applied it to all subjects of knowledge in the giant work after which they were named—the *Encyclopédie*. Thus, in one or the other of its two forms—avowed materialism or deism—it became the creed of the whole cultured youth of France; so much so that, when the great revolution broke out, the doctrine hatched by English Royalists gave a theoretical flag to French Republicans and Terrorists, and furnished the text for the Declaration of the Rights of Man. The great French Revolution was the third uprising of the bourgeoisie, but the first that had entirely cast off the religious cloak and was fought out on undisguised political lines; it was the first, too, that was really fought out up to the destruction of one of the combatants, the aristocracy, and the complete triumph of the other, the bourgeoisie. In England the continuity of pre-revolutionary and post-revolutionary institutions, and the compromise between landlords and capitalists, found its expression in the continuity of judicial precedents and in the religious preservation of the feudal forms of the law. In France the revolution constituted a complete breach with the traditions of the past; it cleared out the very last vestiges of feudalism, and created in the *Code Civil* a masterly adaptation of the old Roman Law—that almost perfect expression of the juridical relations corresponding to the economic stage called by Marx the production of commodities—to modern capitalistic conditions; so masterly that this French revolutionary code still serves as a model for reforms of the law of property in all other countries, not excepting England. Let us, however, not forget that if English law continues to express the economic relations of capitalistic society in that barbarous feudal language which corresponds to the thing expressed, just as English spelling corresponds to English pronunciation—*vous écrivez Londres et vous prononcez Constantinople*, said a Frenchman—that same English law is the only one which has preserved through ages, and transmitted to America and the Colonies the best part of that old Germanic personal freedom, local self-government and independence from all interference but that of the law courts, which on the Continent has been lost during the period of absolute monarchy, and has nowhere been as yet fully recovered.

To return to our British bourgeois. The French Revolution gave him a splendid opportunity, with the help of the Continental monarchies, to destroy French maritime commerce, to annex French colonies, and to crush the last French pretensions to maritime rivalry. That was one reason why he fought it. Another was that the ways of this revolution went very much against his grain. Not only its "execrable" terrorism, but the very attempt to carry bourgeois rule to extremes. What should the British bourgeois do without his aristocracy, that taught him manners, such as they were, and invented fashions for him —that furnished officers for the army, which kept order at home, and the navy, which conquered colonial possessions and new markets abroad? There was indeed a progressive minority of the bourgeoisie, that minority whose interests were not so well attended to under the compromise; this section, composed chiefly of the less wealthy middle class, did sympathise with the revolution, but it was powerless in Parliament.

Thus, if materialism became the creed of the French Revolution, the God-fearing English bourgeois held all the faster to his religion. Had not the reign of terror in Paris proved what was the upshot, if the religious instincts of the masses were lost? The more materialism spread from France to neighbouring countries, and was reinforced by similar doctrinal currents, notably by German philosophy, the more, in fact, materialism and freethought generally became, on the Continent, the necessary qualifications of a cultivated man, the more stubbornly the English middle class stuck to its manifold religious creeds. These creeds might differ from one another, but they were, all of them, distinctly religious, Christian creeds.

While the revolution ensured the political triumph of the bourgeoisie in France, in England Watt, Arkwright, Cartwright, and others, initiated an industrial revolution, which completely shifted the centre of gravity of economic power. The wealth of the bourgeoisie increased considerably faster than that of the landed aristocracy. Within the bourgeoisie itself the financial aristocracy, the bankers, etc., were more and more pushed into the background by the manufacturers. The compromise of 1689, even after the gradual changes it had undergone in favour of the bourgeoisie, no longer corresponded to the relative position of the parties to it. The character of these parties, too, had changed; the bourgeoisie of 1830 was very different from that of the preceding century. The political power still left to the aristocracy, and used by them to resist the pretensions of the new industrial bourgeoisie, became incompatible with the new economic interests. A fresh struggle with the aristocracy was necessary; it could end only in a victory of the new economic power. First, the Reform Act was pushed through, in spite of all resistance, under the impulse of the French Revolution of 1830. It gave to the bourgeoisie a recognised and powerful place in Parliament. Then the repeal of the Corn Laws, which settled, once for all, the supremacy of the bourgeoisie, and especially of its most active portion, the manufacturers, over the landed aristocracy. This was the greatest victory of the bourgeoisie; it was, however, also the last it gained in its own exclusive interest. Whatever triumphs it obtained later on, it had to share with a new social power, first its ally, but soon its rival.

The industrial revolution had created a class of large manufacturing capitalists, but also a class—and a far more numerous one—of manufacturing workpeople. This class gradually increased in numbers, in proportion as the industrial revolution seized upon one branch of manufacture after another, and in the same proportion it increased in power. This power it proved as early as 1824, by forcing a reluctant Parliament to repeal the act forbidding combinations of workmen. During the Reform agitation, the workingmen constituted the Radical wing of the Reform Party; the Act of 1832 having excluded them from the suffrage, they formulated their demands in the People's

Charter, and constituted themselves, in opposition to the great bourgeois Anti-Corn Law party, into an independent party, the Chartists, the first workingmen's party of modern times.

Then came the Continental revolutions of February and March 1848, in which the working people played such a prominent part, and, at least in Paris, put forward demands which were certainly inadmissible from the point of view of capitalist society. And then came the general reaction. First the defeat of the Chartists on the 10th April, 1848, then the crushing of the Paris workingmen's insurrection in June of the same year, then the disasters of 1849 in Italy, Hungary, South Germany, and at last the victory of Louis Bonaparte over Paris, 2nd December, 1851. For a time, at least, the bugbear of working class pretensions was put down, but at what cost! If the British bourgeois had been convinced before of the necessity of maintaining the common people in a religious mood, how much more must he feel that necessity after all these experiences? Regardless of the sneers of his Continental compeers, he continued to spend thousands and tens of thousands, year after year, upon the evangelisation of the lower orders; not content with his own native religious machinery, he appealed to Brother Jonathan, the greatest organiser in existence of religion as a trade, and imported from America revivalism, Moody and Sankey, and the like; and, finally, he accepted the dangerous aid of the Salvation Army, which revives the propaganda of early Christianity, appeals to the poor as the elect, fights capitalism in a religious way, and thus fosters an element of early Christian class antagonism, which one day may become troublesome to the well-to-do people who now find the ready money for it.

It seems a law of historical development that the bourgeoisie can in no European country get hold of political power—at least for any length of time—in the same exclusive way in which the feudal aristocracy kept hold of it during the Middle Ages. Even in France, where feudalism was completely extinguished, the bourgeoisie, as a whole, has held full possession of the government for very short periods only. During Louis Philippe's reign, 1830-48, a very small portion of the bourgeoisie ruled the kingdom; by far the larger part were excluded from the suffrage by the high qualification. Under the second republic, 1848-51, the whole bourgeoisie ruled, but for three years only; their incapacity brought on the second empire. It is only now, in the third republic, that the bourgeoisie as a whole has kept possession of the helm for more than twenty years; and they are already showing lively signs of decadence. A durable reign of the bourgeoisie has been possible only in countries like America, where feudalism was unknown, and society at the very beginning started from a bourgeois basis. And even in France and America, the successors of the bourgeoisie, the working people, are already knocking at the door.

In England, the bourgeoisie never held undivided sway. Even the victory of 1832 left the landed aristocracy in almost exclusive possession of all the leading government offices. The meekness with which the wealthy middle class submitted to this remained inconceivable to me until the great Liberal manufacturer, Mr. W. A. Forster, in a public speech implored the young men of Bradford to learn French, as a means to get on in the world, and quoted from his own experience how sheepish he looked when, as a Cabinet Minister, he had to move in society where French was, at least, as necessary as English! The fact was, the English middle class of that time were, as a rule, quite uneducated upstarts, and could not help leaving to the aristocracy those superior government places where other qualifications were required than mere insular narrowness and insular conceit, seasoned by business sharpness.* Even now the endless news-

* And even in business matters, the conceit of national chauvinism is but a sorry adviser. Up to quite recently, the average English manufacturer considered it derogatory for an Englishman to speak any language but his own, and felt rather proud than otherwise of the fact that "poor devils" of foreigners settled in England and took off his hands the trouble of disposing of his products abroad. He never noticed that these foreigners, mostly Germans, thus got command of a very large part of British foreign trade, imports and exports, and that the direct foreign trade of Englishmen became limited, almost entirely, to the colonies, China, the United States and South America. Nor did he notice that these Germans traded with other Germans abroad, who gradually organised a complete network of commercial colonies all over the world. But when Germany, about forty years ago, seriously began manufacturing for export, this network served her admirably in her transformation, in so short a time, from a corn exporting into a first-rate manufacturing coun-

paper debates about middle class education show that the English middle class does not yet consider itself good enough for the best education, and looks to something more modest. Thus, even after the repeal of the Corn Laws, it appeared a matter of course, that the men who had carried the day, the Cobdens, Brights, Forsters, etc. should remain excluded from a share in the official government of the country, until twenty years afterwards, a new Reform Act opened to them the door of the Cabinet. The English bourgeoisie are, up to the present day, so deeply penetrated by a sense of their social inferiority that they keep up, at their own expense and that of the nation, an ornamental caste of drones to represent the nation worthily at all state functions; and they consider themselves highly honoured whenever one of themselves is found worthy of admission into this select and privileged body, manufactured, after all, by themselves.

The industrial and commercial middle class had, therefore, not yet succeeded in driving the landed aristocracy completely from political power when another competitor, the working class, appeared on the stage. The reaction after the Chartist movement and the Continental revolutions, as well as the unparalleled extension of English trade from 1848-66 (ascribed vulgarly to Free Trade alone, but due far more to the colossal development of railways, ocean steamers and means of intercourse generally), had again driven the working class into the dependency of the Liberal Party, of which they formed, as in pre-Chartist times, the radical wing. Their claims to the franchise, however, gradually became irresistible; while the Whig leaders of the Liberals "funked," Disraeli showed his superiority by making the Tories seize the favourable moment and introduce household suffrage in the boroughs, along with a redistribution of seats. Then followed the ballot; then in 1884 the extension of household suffrage to the counties and a fresh redistribu-

---

try. Then, about ten years ago, the British manufacturer got frightened, and asked his ambassadors and consuls how it was that he could no longer keep his customers together. The unanimous answer was: 1) You don't learn your customer's language but expect him to speak your own: 2) You don't even try to suit your customer's wants, habits, and tastes, but expect him to conform to your English ones.

tion of seats, by which electoral districts were to some extent equalised. All these measures considerably increased the electoral power of the working class, so much so that in at least 150 to 200 constituencies that class now furnishes the majority of voters. But parliamentary government is a capital school for teaching respect for tradition; if the middle class look with awe and veneration upon what Lord John Manners playfully called "our old nobility," the mass of the working people then looked up with respect and deference to what used to be designated as "their betters," the middle class. Indeed, the British workman, some fifteen years ago, was the model workman, whose respectful regard for the position of his master, and whose self-restraining modesty in claiming rights for himself, consoled our German economists of the *Katheder-Socialist* * school for the incurable communistic and revolutionary tendencies of their own working men at home.

But the English middle class—good men of business as they are—saw farther than the German professors. They had shared their power but reluctantly with the working class. They had learnt, during the Chartist years, what that *puer robustus sed malitiosus,* the people, is capable of. And since that time, they had been compelled to incorporate the better part of the People's Charter in the Statutes of the United Kingdom. Now, if ever, the people must be kept in order by moral means, and the first and foremost of all moral means of action upon the masses is and remains—religion. Hence the parsons' majorities on the School Boards, hence the increasing self-taxation of the bourgeoisie for the support of all sorts of revivalism from ritualism to the Salvation Army.

And now came the triumph of British respectability over the free thought and religious laxity of the Continental bourgeois. The workmen of France and Germany had become rebellious. They were thoroughly infected with socialism, and, for very good reasons, were not at all particular as to the legality of the means by which to secure their own ascendency. The *puer robustus,* here, turned from day to day more *malitiosus.* Nothing remained to the French and German bourgeoisie as a last resource but to silently drop their free thought, as a

* Professorial Socialist.—*Ed.*

youngster, when sea-sickness creeps upon him, quietly drops
the burning cigar he brought swaggeringly on board; one by
one, the scoffers turned pious in outward behaviour, spoke with
respect of the Church, its dogmas and rites, and even conformed
with the latter as far as could not be helped. French bourgeoisie
dined *maigre* on Fridays, and German ones sat out long
Protestant sermons in their pews on Sundays. They had come
to grief with materialism. *"Die Religion muss dem Volk
erhalten werden,"*—religion must be kept alive for the people—
that was the only and the last means to save society from utter
ruin. Unfortunately for themselves, they did not find this out
until they had done their level best to break up religion for ever.
And now it was the turn of the British bourgeois to sneer and
to say: "Why, you fools, I could have told you that two hundred
years ago!"

However, I am afraid neither the religious stolidity of the
British, nor the *post festum* conversion of the Continental
bourgeois will stem the rising proletarian tide. Tradition is a
great retarding force, is the *vis inertiæ* of history, but, being
merely passive, is sure to be broken down; and thus religion
will be no lasting safeguard to capitalist society. If our juridical,
philosophical and religious ideas are the more or less remote
offshoots of the economical relations prevailing in a given
society, such ideas cannot, in the long run, withstand the effects
of a complete change in these relations. And, unless we believe
in supernatural revelation, we must admit that no religious tenets
will ever suffice to prop up a tottering society.

In fact, in England too, the working people have begun to
move again. They are, no doubt, shackled by traditions of
various kinds. Bourgeois traditions, such as the widespread
belief that there can be but two parties, Conservatives and
Liberals, and that the working class must work out its salvation
by and through the great Liberal Party. Workingmen's traditions, inherited from their first tentative efforts at independent
action, such as the exclusion, from ever so many old trade
unions, of all applicants who have not gone through a regular
apprenticeship; which means the breeding, by every such union,
of its own blacklegs. But for all that the English working class
is moving, as even Professor Brentano has sorrowfully had to

report to his brother *Katheder-Socialists.* It moves, like all things in England, with a slow and measured step, with hesitation here, with more or less unfruitful, tentative attempts there; it moves now and then with an over-cautious mistrust of the name of socialism, while it gradually absorbs the substance; and the movement spreads and seizes one layer of the workers after another. It has now shaken out of their torpor the unskilled labourers of the East End of London, and we all know what a splendid impulse these fresh forces have given it in return. And if the pace of the movement is not up to the impatience of some people, let them not forget that it is the working class which keeps alive the finest qualities of the English character, and that, if a step in advance is once gained in England, it is, as a rule, never lost afterwards. If the sons of the old Chartists, for reasons explained above, were not quite up to the mark, the grandsons bid fair to be worthy of their forefathers.

But the triumph of the European working class does not depend upon England alone. It can only be secured by the co-operation of, at least, England, France and Germany. In both the latter countries the working class movement is well ahead of England. In Germany it is even within measurable distance of success. The progress it has there made during the last twenty-five years is unparalleled. It advances with ever increasing velocity. If the German middle class have shown themselves lamentably deficient in political capacity, discipline, courage, energy and perseverance, the German working class have given ample proof of all these qualities. Four hundred years ago, Germany was the starting point of the first upheaval of the European middle class; as things are now, is it outside the limits of possibility that Germany will be the scene, too, of the first great victory of the European proletariat?

April 20, 1892   F. ENGELS

SOCIALISM
UTOPIAN AND SCIENTIFIC

I

MODERN SOCIALISM is, in its essence, the direct product of the recognition, on the one hand, of the class antagonisms, existing in the society of today, between proprietors and non-proprietors, between capitalists and wage workers; on the other hand, of the anarchy existing in production. But, in its theoretical form, modern socialism originally appears ostensibly as a more logical extension of the principles laid down by the great French philosophers of the eighteenth century. Like every new theory, modern socialism had, at first, to connect itself with the intellectual stock-in-trade ready to its hand, however deeply its roots lay in material economic facts.

The great men, who in France prepared men's minds for the coming revolution, were themselves extreme revolutionists. They recognised no external authority of any kind whatever. Religion, natural science, society, political institutions, everything, was subjected to the most unsparing criticism: everything must justify its existence before the judgment seat of reason, or give up existence. Reason became the sole measure of everything. It was the time when, as Hegel says, the world stood upon its head; * first, in the sense that the human head, and

* This is the passage on the French Revolution: "Thought, the concept of law, all at once made itself felt, and against this the old scaffolding of wrong could make no stand. In this conception of law, therefore, a constitution has now been established, and henceforth everything must be based upon this. Since the sun had been in the firmament, and the planets circled round him, the sight had never been seen of man standing upon his head—i.e., on the idea—and building reality after this image. Anaxagoras first said that the *Nous*, reason, rules the world; but now, for the first time, had man come to recognise that the Idea must rule the mental reality. And this was a magnificent sunrise. All thinking

the principles arrived at by its thought, claimed to be the basis of all human action and association; but by and by, also, in the wider sense that the reality which was in contradiction to these principles had, in fact, to be turned upside down. Every form of society and government then existing, every old traditional notion was flung into the lumber room as irrational; the world had hitherto allowed itself to be led solely by prejudices; everything in the past deserved only pity and contempt. Now, for the first time, appeared the light of day, the kingdom of reason; henceforth superstition, injustice, privilege, oppression, were to be superseded by eternal truth, eternal right, equality based on nature and the inalienable rights of man.

We know today that this kingdom of reason was nothing more than the idealised kingdom of the bourgeoisie; that this eternal right found its realisation in bourgeois justice; that this equality reduced itself to bourgeois equality before the law; that bourgeois property was proclaimed as one of the essential rights of man; and that the government of reason, the *Contrat Social* of Rousseau, came into being, and only could come into being, as a democratic bourgeois republic. The great thinkers of the eighteenth century could, no more than their predecessors, go beyond the limits imposed upon them by their epoch.

But, side by side with the antagonism of the feudal nobility and the burghers, who claimed to represent all the rest of society, was the general antagonism of exploiters and exploited, of rich idlers and poor workers. It was this very circumstance that made it possible for the representatives of the bourgeoisie to put themselves forward as representing not one special class, but the whole of suffering humanity. Still further. From its origin, the bourgeoisie was saddled with its antithesis: capitalists cannot exist without wage workers, and, in the same proportion as the mediæval burgher of the guild developed into the modern bourgeois, the guild journeyman and the day labourer, outside

beings have participated in celebrating this holy day. A sublime emotion swayed men at that time, an enthusiasm of reason pervaded the world, as if now had come the reconciliation of the Divine Principle with the world." [Hegel: *Philosophy of History*, 1840, p. 535.] Is it not high time to set the Anti-Socialist Law in action against such teachings, subversive and to the common danger, by the late Professor Hegel?

the guilds, developed into the proletarian. And although, upon the whole, the bourgeoisie, in their struggle with the nobility, could claim to represent at the same time the interests of the different working classes of that period, yet in every great bourgeois movement there were independent outbursts of that class which was the forerunner, more or less developed, of the modern proletariat. For example, at the time of the German reformation and the peasants' war, the Anabaptists and Thomas Münzer; in the great English Revolution, the Levellers; in the great French Revolution, Babœuf.

There were theoretical enunciations corresponding with these revolutionary uprisings of a class not yet developed; in the sixteenth and seventeenth centuries, utopian pictures of ideal social conditions; in the eighteenth, actual communistic theories (Morelly and Mably). The demand for equality was no longer limited to political rights; it was extended also to the social conditions of individuals. It was not simply class privileges that were to be abolished, but class distinctions themselves. A communism, ascetic, denouncing all the pleasures of life, Spartan, was the first form of the new teaching. Then came the three great Utopians: Saint Simon, to whom the middle class movement, side by side with the proletarian, still had a certain significance; Fourier; and Owen, who in the country where capitalist production was most developed, and under the influence of the antagonisms begotten of this, worked out his proposals for the removal of class distinction systematically and in direct relation to French materialism.

One thing is common to all three. Not one of them appears as a representative of the interests of that proletariat, which historical development had in the meantime produced. Like the French philosophers, they do not claim to emancipate a particular class to begin with, but all humanity at once. Like them, they wish to bring in the kingdom of reason and eternal justice, but this kingdom, as they see it, is as far as heaven from earth from that of the French philosophers.

For, to our three social reformers, the bourgeois world, based upon the principles of these philosophers, is quite as irrational and unjust, and, therefore, finds its way to the dust hole quite as readily as feudalism and all the earlier stages of

society. If pure reason and justice have not, hitherto, ruled
the world, this has been the case only because men have not
rightly understood them. What was wanted was the individual
man of genius, who has now arisen and who understands the
truth. That he has now arisen, that the truth has now been
clearly understood, is not an inevitable event, following of
necessity in the chain of historical development, but a mere
happy accident. He might just as well have been born 500
years earlier, and might then have spared humanity 500 years
of error, strife and suffering.

We saw how the French philosophers of the eighteenth century, the forerunners of the revolution, appealed to reason as
the sole judge of all that is. A rational government, rational
society, were to be founded; everything that ran counter to
eternal reason was to be remorselessly done away with. We
saw also that this eternal reason was in reality nothing but the
idealised understanding of the eighteenth century citizen, just
then evolving into the bourgeois. The French Revolution had
realised this rational society and government.

But the new order of things, rational enough as compared
with earlier conditions, turned out to be by no means absolutely
rational. The state based upon reason completely collapsed.
Rousseau's *Contrat Social* had found its realisation in the Reign
of Terror, from which bourgeoisie, who had lost confidence
in their own political capacity, had taken refuge first in the
corruption of the Directorate, and, finally, under the wing of
the Napoleonic despotism. The promised eternal peace was
turned into an endless war of conquest. The society based upon
reason had fared no better. The antagonism between rich and
poor, instead of dissolving into general prosperity, had become
intensified by the removal of the guild and other privileges,
which had to some extent bridged it over, and by the removal
of the charitable institutions of the Church. The "freedom of
property" from feudal fetters, now veritably accomplished,
turned out to be, for the small capitalists and small proprietors,
the freedom to sell their small property, crushed under the
overmastering competition of the large capitalists and landlords,
to these great lords, and thus, as far as the small capitalists
and peasant proprietors were concerned, became "freedom *from*

property." The development of industry upon a capitalistic basis made poverty and misery of the working masses conditions of existence of society. Cash payment became more and more, in Carlyle's phrase, the sole nexus between man and man. The number of crimes increased from year to year. Formerly, the feudal vices had openly stalked about in broad daylight; though not eradicated, they were now at any rate thrust into the background. In their stead, the bourgeois vices, hitherto practised in secret, began to blossom all the more luxuriantly. Trade became to a greater and greater extent cheating. The "fraternity" of the revolutionary motto was realized in the chicanery and rivalries of the battle of competition. Oppression by force was replaced by corruption; the sword, as the first social lever, by gold. The right of the first night was transferred from the feudal lords to the bourgeois manufacturers. Prostitution increased to an extent never heard of. Marriage itself remained, as before, the legally recognised form, the official cloak of prostitution, and, moreover, was supplemented by rich crops of adultery.

In a word, compared with the splendid promises of the philosophers, the social and political institutions born of the "triumph of reason" were bitterly disappointing caricatures. All that was wanting was the men to formulate this disappointment, and they came with the turn of the century. In 1802 Saint Simon's Geneva Letters appeared; in 1808 appeared Fourier's first work, although the groundwork of his theory dated from 1799; on January 1, 1800, Robert Owen undertook the direction of New Lanark.

At this time, however, the capitalist mode of production, and with it the antagonism between the bourgeoisie and the proletariat, was still very incompletely developed. Modern industry, which had just arisen in England, was still unknown in France. But modern industry develops, on the one hand, the conflicts which make absolutely necessary a revolution in the mode of production and the doing away with its capitalistic character— conflicts not only between the classes begotten of it, but also between the very productive forces and the forms of exchange created by it. And, on the other hand, it develops, in these very gigantic productive forces, the means of ending these conflicts.

If, therefore, about the year 1800, the conflicts arising from the new social order were only just beginning to take shape, this holds still more fully as to the means of ending them. The "have-nothing" masses of Paris, during the Reign of Terror, were able for a moment to gain the mastery, and thus to lead the bourgeois revolution to victory in spite of the bourgeoisie themselves. But, in doing so, they only proved how impossible it was for their domination to last under the conditions then obtaining. The proletariat, which then for the first time evolved itself from these "have-nothing" masses as the nucleus of a new class, as yet quite incapable of independent political action, appeared as an oppressed, suffering order, to whom, in its incapacity to help itself, help could, at best, he brought in from without or down from above.

This historical situation also dominated the founders of socialism. To the crude conditions of capitalistic production and the crude class conditions corresponded crude theories. The solution of the social problems, which as yet lay hidden in undeveloped economic conditions, the utopians attempted to evolve out of the human brain. Society presented nothing but wrongs; to remove these was the task of reason. It was necessary, then, to discover a new and more perfect system of social order and to impose this upon society from without by propaganda, and, wherever it was possible, by the example of model experiments. These new social systems were foredoomed as utopian; the more completely they were worked out in detail, the more they could not avoid drifting off into pure phantasies.

These facts once established, we need not dwell a moment longer upon this side of the question, now wholly belonging to the past. We can leave it to the literary small fry to solemnly quibble over these phantasies, which today only make us smile, and to crow over the superiority of their own bald reasoning, as compared with such "insanity." For ourselves, we delight in the stupendously grand thoughts and germs of thought that everywhere break out through their phantastic covering, and to which these philistines are blind.

Saint Simon was a son of the great French Revolution, at the outbreak of which he was not yet thirty. The revolution was the victory of the third estate, *i.e.*, of the great masses of the nation, *working* in production and in trade over the privileged *idle* classes, the nobles and the priests. But the victory of the third estate soon revealed itself as exclusively the victory of a small part of this "estate," as the conquest of political power by the socially privileged section of it, *i.e.*, the propertied bourgeoisie. And the bourgeoisie had certainly developed rapidly during the revolution, partly by speculation in the lands of the nobility and of the Church, confiscated and afterwards put up for sale, and partly by frauds upon the nation by means of army contracts. It was the domination of these swindlers that, under the Directorate, brought France to the verge of ruin, and thus gave Napoleon the pretext for his *coup d'état*.

Hence, to Saint Simon the antagonism between the third estate and the privileged classes took the form of an antagonism between "workers" and "idlers." The idlers were not merely the old privileged classes, but also all who, without taking any part in production or distribution, lived on their incomes. And the workers were not only the wage workers, but also the manufacturers, the merchants, the bankers. That the idlers had lost the capacity for intellectual leadership and political supremacy had been proved, and was by the revolution finally settled. That the non-possessing classes had not this capacity seemed to Saint Simon proved by the experiences of the Reign of Terror. Then, who was to lead and command? According to Saint Simon, science and industry, both united by a new religious bond, destined to restore that unity of religious ideas which had been lost since the time of the Reformation—a necessarily mystic and rigidly hierarchic "new Christianity." But science, that was the scholars; and industry, that was, in the first place, the working bourgeois, manufacturers, merchants, bankers. These bourgeoisie were, certainly, intended by Saint Simon to transform themselves into a kind of public officials, of social trustees; but they were still to hold, *vis-à-vis* of the workers, a commanding and economically privileged position. The bankers especially were to be called upon to direct the whole of social production by the regulation of credit. This conception was in exact keeping with a time in which modern industry in France and, with it, the chasm between bourgeoisie and proletariat was only just coming into existence. But what Saint Simon especially lays stress upon is this: what interests him first, and above all other things, is the lot of the class that is the most numerous and the most poor (*"la classe la plus nombreuse et la plus pauvre"*).

Already, in his Geneva Letters, Saint Simon lays down the proposition that "all men ought to work." In the same work he recognises also that the Reign of Terror was the reign of the non-possessing masses. "See," says he to them, "what happened in France at the time when your comrades held sway there; they brought about a famine." But to recognise the French Revolution as a class war, and not simply one between nobility and bourgeoisie, but between nobility, bourgeoisie and the non-possessors, was, in the year 1802, a most pregnant discovery. In 1816 he declares that politics is the science of production, and foretells the complete absorption of politics by economics. The knowledge that economic conditions are the basis of political institutions appears here only in embryo. Yet what is here already very plainly expressed is the idea of the future conversion of political rule over men into an administration of things and a direction of processes of production—that is to say, the "abolition of the state," about which recently there has been so much noise.

Saint Simon shows the same superiority over his contemporaries, when in 1814, immediately after the entry of the allies into Paris, and again in 1815, during the Hundred Days' War, he proclaims the alliance of France with England, and then of both these countries with Germany, as the only guarantee for the prosperous development and peace of Europe. To preach to the French in 1815 an alliance with the victors of Waterloo required as much courage as historical foresight.

If in Saint Simon we find a comprehensive breadth of view, by virtue of which almost all the ideas of later socialists, that are not strictly economic, are found in him in embryo, we find in Fourier a criticism of the existing conditions of society, genuinely French and witty, but not upon that account any the less thorough. Fourier takes the bourgeoisie, their inspired prophets before the revolution, and their interested eulogists after it, at their own word. He lays bare remorselessly the material and moral misery of the bourgeois world. He confronts it with the earlier philosophers' dazzling promises of a society in which reason alone should reign, of a civilisation in which happiness should be universal, of an illimitable human perfectibility, and with the rose-coloured phraseology of the bourgeois ideologists of his time. He points out how everywhere the most pitiful reality corresponds with the most high-sounding phrases, and he overwhelms this hopeless fiasco of phrases with his mordant sarcasm.

Fourier is not only a critic; his imperturbably serene nature makes him a satirist, and assuredly one of the greatest satirists of all time. He depicts, with equal power and charm, the swindling speculations that blossomed out upon the downfall of the revolution, and the shopkeeping spirit prevalent in, and characteristic of, French commerce at that time. Still more masterly is his criticism of the bourgeois form of the relations between the sexes, and the position of woman in bourgeois society. He was the first to declare that in any given society the degree of woman's emancipation is the natural measure of the general emancipation.

But Fourier is at his greatest in his conception of the history of society. He divides its whole course, thus far, into four stages of evolution—savagery, barbarism, the patriarchate, civilisation. This last is identical with the so-called civil, or bourgeois society of today—i.e., with the social order that came in with the sixteenth century. He proves "that the civilised stage raises every vice practised by barbarism in a simple fashion, into a form of existence, complex, ambiguous, equivocal, hypocritical"—that civilisation moves in "a vicious circle," in contradictions which it constantly reproduces without being able to solve them; hence it constantly arrives at the very opposite to that which it wants to attain, or pretends to want to attain, so that, e.g., "under civilisation poverty is born of superabundance itself."

Fourier, as we see, uses the dialectic method in the same masterly way as his contemporary, Hegel. Using these same dialectics, he argues against the talk about illimitable human perfectibility that every historical phase has its period of ascent and also its period of descent, and he applies this observation

to the future of the whole human race. As Kant introduced
into natural science the idea of the ultimate destruction of the
earth, Fourier introduced into historical science that of the
ultimate destruction of the human race.

Whilst in France the hurricane of the revolution swept over
the land, in England a quieter, but not on that account less
tremendous, revolution was going on. Steam and the new tool-
making machinery were transforming manufacture into modern
industry, and thus revolutionising the whole foundation of bourgeois society. The sluggish march of development of the
manufacturing period changed into a veritable storm and stress
period of production. With constantly increasing swiftness
the splitting-up of society into large capitalists and non-possessing proletarians went on. Between these, instead of the former
stable middle class, an unstable mass of artisans and small shop-
keepers, the most fluctuating portion of the population, now
led a precarious existence.

The new mode of production was, as yet, only at the beginning of its period of ascent; as yet it was the normal, regular
method of production—the only one possible under existing
conditions. Nevertheless, even then it was producing crying
social abuses—the herding together of a homeless population
in the worst quarters of the large towns; the loosening of all
traditional moral bonds, of patriarchal subordination, of family
relations; overwork, especially of women and children, to a
frightful extent; complete demoralisation of the working class,
suddenly flung into altogether new conditions, from the country
into the town, from agriculture into modern industry, from
stable conditions of existence into insecure ones that changed
from day to day.

At this juncture there came forward as a reformer a manufacturer 29 years old—a man of almost sublime, childlike sim-
plicity of character, and at the same time one of the few born
leaders of men. Robert Owen had adopted the teaching of the
materialistic philosophers: that man's character is the product,
on the one hand, of heredity, on the other, of the environment
of the individual during his lifetime, and especially during his
period of development. In the industrial revolution most of his

class saw only chaos and confusion, and the opportunity of fishing in these troubled waters and making large fortunes quickly. He saw in it the opportunity of putting into practice his favourite theory, and so of bringing order out of chaos. He had already tried it with success, as superintendent of more than five hundred men in a Manchester factory. From 1800 to 1829, he directed the great cotton mill at New Lanark, in Scotland, as managing partner, along the same lines, but with greater freedom of action and with a success that made him a European reputation. A population, originally consisting of the most diverse and, for the most part, very demoralised elements, a population that gradually grew to 2,500, he turned into a model colony, in which drunkenness, police, magistrates, lawsuits, poor laws, charity were unknown. And all this simply by placing the people in conditions worthy of human beings, and especially by carefully bringing up the rising generation. He was the founder of infant schools, and introduced them first at New Lanark. At the age of two the children came to school, where they enjoyed themselves so much that they could scarcely be got home again. Whilst his competitors worked their people thirteen or fourteen hours a day, in New Lanark the working day was only ten and a half hours. When a crisis in cotton stopped work for four months, his workers received their full wages all the time. And with all this the business more than doubled in value, and to the last yielded large profits to its proprietors.

In spite of all this, Owen was not content. The existence which he secured for his workers was, in his eyes, still far from being worthy of human beings. "The people were slaves at my mercy." The relatively favourable conditions in which he had placed them were still far from allowing a rational development of the character and of the intellect in all directions, much less of the free exercise of all their faculties. "And yet, the working part of this population of 2,500 persons was daily producing as much real wealth for society as, less than half a century before, it would have required the working part of a population of 600,000 to create. I asked myself, what became of the difference between the wealth consumed by 2,500 persons and that which would have been consumed by 600,000?" *

The answer was clear. It had been used to pay the proprietors of the establishment 5 per cent on the capital they had laid out, in addition to over £300,000 clear profit. And that which held for New Lanark held to a still greater extent for all the factories in England. "If this new wealth had not been created by machinery, imperfectly as it has been applied, the wars of Europe, in opposition to Napoleon, and to support the aristocratic principles of society, could not have been maintained. And yet this new power was the creation of the working classes." ** To them, therefore, the fruits of this new power belonged. The newly-created, gigantic productive forces, hitherto used only to enrich individuals and to enslave the masses, offered to Owen the foundations for a reconstruction of society; they were destined, as the common property of all, to be worked for the common good of all.

Owen's communism was based upon this purely business foundation, the outcome, so to say, of commercial calculation. Throughout, it maintained this practical character. Thus, in 1823, Owen proposed the relief of the distress in Ireland by communist colonies, and drew up complete estimates of costs of founding them, yearly expenditure and probable revenue. And in his definite plan for the future, the technical working out of details is managed with such practical knowledge—ground plan, front and side and bird's-eye views all included—that the Owen method of social reform once accepted, there is from the practical point of view little to be said against the actual arrangement of details.

His advance in the direction of communism was the turning-point in Owen's life. As long as he was simply a philanthropist, he was rewarded with nothing but wealth, applause, honour and glory. He was the most popular man in Europe. Not only men of his own class, but statesmen and princes listened to him

* From *The Revolution in Mind and Practice*, p. 21, a memorial addressed to all the "red republicans, communists and socialists of Europe," and sent to the provisional government of France, 1848, and also "to Queen Victoria and her responsible advisers."
** *Ibid.*

approvingly. But when he came out with his communist theories, that was quite another thing. Three great obstacles seemed to him especially to block the path to social reform: private property, religion, the present form of marriage. He knew what confronted him if he attacked these—outlawry, excommunication from official society, the loss of his whole social position. But nothing of this prevented him from attacking them without fear of consequences, and what he had foreseen happened. Banished from official society, with a conspiracy of silence against him in the press, ruined by his unsuccessful communist experiments in America, in which he sacrificed all his fortune, he turned directly to the working class and continued working in their midst for thirty years. Every social movement, every real advance in England on behalf of the workers links itself on to the name of Robert Owen. He forced through in 1819, after five years' fighting, the first law limiting the hours of labour of women and children in factories. He was president of the first congress at which all the trade unions of England united in a single great trade association. He introduced as transition measures to the complete communistic organisation of society, on the one hand, co-operative societies for retail trade and production. These have since that time, at least, given practical proof that the merchant and the manufacturer are socially quite unnecessary. On the other hand, he introduced labour bazaars for the exchange of the products of labour through the medium of labour notes, whose unit was a single hour of work; institutions necessarily doomed to failure, but completely anticipating Proudhon's bank of exchange of a much later period, and differing entirely from this in that it did not claim to be the panacea for all social ills, but only a first step towards a much more radical revolution of society.

The Utopians' mode of thought has for a long time governed the socialist ideas of the nineteenth century, and still governs some of them. Until very recently all French and English socialists did homage to it. The earlier German communism, including that of Weitling, was of the same school. To all these, socialism is the expression of absolute truth, reason and justice, and has only to be discovered to conquer all the world by virtue of its own power. And as absolute truth is independent of time, space, and of the historical development of man, it is a mere accident when and where it is discovered. With all this, absolute truth, reason and justice are different with the founder of each different school. And as each one's special kind of absolute truth, reason and justice is again conditioned by his subjective understanding, his conditions of existence, the measure of his knowledge and his intellectual training, there is no other ending possible in this conflict of absolute truths than that they shall be mutually exclusive one of the other. Hence, from this nothing could come but a kind of eclectic, average socialism, which, as a matter of fact, has up to the present time dominated the minds of most of the socialist workers in France and England. Hence, a mish-mash allowing of the most manifold shades of opinion; a mish-mash of such critical statements, economic theories, pictures of future society by the founders of different sects, as excite a minimum of opposition; a mish-mash which is the more easily brewed the more the definite sharp edges of the individual constituents are rubbed down in the stream of debate, like rounded pebbles in a brook.

To make a science of socialism, it had first to be placed upon a real basis.

H.m.

II

In the meantime, along with and after the French philosophy of the eighteenth century had arisen the new German philosophy, culminating in Hegel. Its greatest merit was the taking up again of dialectics as the highest form of reasoning. The old Greek philosophers were all born natural dialecticians, and Aristotle, the most encyclopædic intellect of them, had already analysed the most essential forms of dialectic thought. The newer philosophy, on the other hand, although in it also dialectics had brilliant exponents (e.g. Descartes and Spinoza), had, especially through English influence, become more and more rigidly fixed in the so-called metaphysical mode of reasoning, by which also the French of the eighteenth century were almost wholly dominated, at all events in their special philosophical work. Outside philosophy in the restricted sense, the French nevertheless produced masterpieces of dialectic. We need only call to mind Diderot's *Le Neveu de Rameau,* and Rousseau's *Discours sur l'origine et les fondements de l'inégalité parmi les hommes.* We give here, in brief, the essential character of these two modes of thought.

When we consider and reflect upon nature at large, or the history of mankind, or our own intellectual activity, at first we see the picture of an endless entanglement of relations and reactions, permutations and combinations, in which nothing remains what, where, and as it was, but everything moves, changes, comes into being and passes away. We see, therefore, at first the picture as a whole, with its individual parts still more or less kept in the background; we observe the movements, transitions, connections, rather than the things that move, combine, and are connected. This primitive, naïve, but intrinsically correct conception of the world is that of ancient Greek philosophy, and was first clearly formulated by Heraclitus : everything is and is not, for everything is fluid, is constantly changing, constantly coming into being and passing away.

But this conception, correctly as it expresses the general character of the picture of appearances as a whole, does not suffice to explain the details of which this picture is made up, and so long as we do not understand these, we have not a clear idea of the whole picture. In order to understand these details we must detach them from their natural or historical connection and examine each one separately, its nature, special causes, effects, etc. This is, primarily, the task of natural science and historical research; branches of science which the Greeks of classical times, on very good grounds, relegated to a subordinate position, because they had first of all to collect materials for these sciences to work upon. A certain amount of natural and historical material must be collected before there can be any critical analysis, comparison and arrangement in classes, orders and species. The foundations of the exact natural sciences were, therefore, first worked out by the Greeks of the Alexandrian period, and later on, in the Middle Ages, by the Arabs. Real natural science dates from the second half of the fifteenth century, and thence onward it has advanced with constantly increasing rapidity. The analysis of nature into its individual parts, the grouping of the different natural processes and objects in definite classes, the study of the internal anatomy of organised bodies in their manifold forms—these were the fundamental conditions of the gigantic strides in our knowledge of nature that have been made during the last four hundred years. But this method of work has also left us as legacy the habit of observing natural objects and processes in isolation, apart from their connection with the vast whole; of observing them in repose, not in motion; as constants, not as essentially variables; in their death, not in their life. And when this way of looking at things was transferred by Bacon and Locke from natural science to philosophy, it begot the narrow, metaphysical mode of thought peculiar to the last century.

To the metaphysician, things and their mental reflexes, ideas, are isolated, are to be considered one after the other and apart from each other, are objects of investigation fixed, rigid, given once for all. He thinks in absolutely irreconcilable antitheses. "His communication is 'yea, yea; nay, nay'; for whatsoever is more than these cometh of evil." For him a thing either exists or does not exist; a thing cannot at the same time be itself and something else. Positive and negative absolutely exclude one another; cause and effect stand in a rigid antithesis one to the other.

At first sight this mode of thinking seems to us very luminous, because it is that of so-called sound common sense. Only sound common sense, respectable fellow that he is, in the homely realm of his own four walls, has very wonderful adventures directly he ventures out into the wide world of research. And the metaphysical mode of thought, justifiable and necessary as it is in a number of domains whose extent varies according to the nature of the particular object of investigation, sooner or later reaches a limit, beyond which it becomes one-sided, restricted, abstract, lost in insoluble contradictions. In the contemplation of individual things, it forgets the connection between them; in the contemplation of their existence, it forgets the beginning and end of that existence; of their repose, it forgets their motion. It cannot see the wood for the trees.

For everyday purposes we know and can say, e.g., whether an animal is alive or not. But, upon closer inquiry, we find that this is, in many cases, a very complex question, as the jurists know very well. They have cudgelled their brains in vain to discover a rational limit beyond which the killing of the child in its mother's womb is murder. It is just as impossible to determine absolutely the moment of death, for physiology proves that death is not an instantaneous, momentary phenomenon, but a very protracted process.

In like manner, every organised being is every moment the same and not the same; every moment it assimilates matter supplied from without, and gets rid of other matter; every moment some cells of its body die and others build themselves anew; in a longer or shorter time the matter of its body is completely renewed, and is replaced by other molecules of matter, so that every organised being is always itself, and yet something other than itself.

Further, we find upon closer investigation that the two poles of an antithesis, positive and negative, e.g., are as inseparable as they are opposed, and that despite all their opposition, they mutually interpenetrate. And we find, in like manner, that cause and effect are conceptions which only hold good in their application to individual cases; but as soon as we consider the individual cases in their general connection with the universe as a whole, they run into each other, and they become confounded when we contemplate that universal action and reaction in which causes and effects are eternally changing places, so that what is effect here and now will be cause there and then, and *vice versa*.

None of these processes and modes of thought enters into the framework of metaphysical reasoning. Dialectics, on the other hands, comprehends things and their representations, ideas, in their essential connection, concatenation, motion, origin and ending. Such processes as those mentioned above are, therefore, so many corroborations of its own method of procedure.

Nature is the proof of dialectics, and it must be said for modern science that it has furnished this proof with very rich materials increasing daily, and thus has shown that, in the last resort, nature works dialectically and not metaphysically; that she does not move in the eternal oneness of a perpetually recurring circle, but goes through a real historical evolution. In this connection Darwin must be named before all others. He dealt the metaphysical conception of nature the heaviest blow by his proof that all organic beings, plants, animals and man himself, are the products of a process of evolution going on through millions of years. But the naturalists who have learned to think dialectically are few and far between, and this conflict of the results of discovery with preconceived modes of thinking explains the endless confusion now reigning in theoretical natural science, the despair of teachers as well as learners, of authors and readers alike.

An exact representation of the universe, of its evolution, of the development of mankind, and of the reflection of this evolution in the minds of men, can therefore only be obtained by the methods of dialectics, with its constant regard to the innumerable actions and reactions of life and death, of progressive or retrogressive changes. And in this spirit the new German philosophy has worked. Kant began his career by resolving the stable solar system of Newton and its eternal duration, after the famous initial impulse had once been given, into the result of a historic process, the formation of the sun and all the planets out of a rotating nebulous mass. From this he at the same time drew the conclusion that, given this origin of the solar system, its future death followed of necessity. His theory half a century later was established mathematically by Laplace, and half a century after that the spectroscope proved the existence in space of such incandescent masses of gas in various stages of condensation.

This new German philosophy culminated in the Hegelian system. In this system—and herein is its great merit—for the first time the whole world, natural, historical, intellectual, is represented as a process, *i.e.,* as in constant motion, change, transformation, development; and the attempt is made to trace out the internal connection that makes a continuous whole of all this movement and development. From this point of view the history of mankind no longer appeared as a wild whirl of senseless deeds of violence, all equally condemnable at the judgment seat of mature philosophic reason, and which are best forgotten as quickly as possible, but as the process of evolution of man himself. It was now the task of the intellect to follow the gradual march of this process through all its devious ways, and to trace out the inner law running through all its apparently accidental phenomena.

That the Hegelian system did not solve the problem it propounded is here immaterial. Its epoch-making merit was that it propounded the problem. This problem is one that no single individual will ever be able to solve. Although Hegel was—with Saint Simon—the most encyclopædic mind of his time, yet he was limited, first, by the necessarily limited extent of his own knowledge, and, second, by the limited extent and depth of the knowledge and conceptions of his age. To these limits a third must be added. Hegel was an idealist. To him the thoughts within his brain were not the more or less abstract pictures of actual things and processes, but, conversely, things and their evolution were only the realised pictures of the "Idea," existing somewhere from eternity before the world was. This way of thinking turned everything upside down, and completely reversed the actual connection of things in the world. Correctly and ingeniously as many individual groups of facts were grasped by Hegel, yet, for the reasons just given, there is much that is botched, artificial, laboured, in a word, wrong in point of detail. The Hegelian system, in itself, was a colossal miscarriage—but it was also the last of its kind. It was suffering, in fact, from an internal and incurable contradiction. Upon the one hand, its essential proposition was the conception that human history is a process of evolution, which, by its very nature, cannot find its intellectual final term in the discovery of any so-called absolute truth. But, on the other hand, it laid claim to being the very essence of this absolute truth. A system of natural and historical knowledge embracing everything, and final for all time, is a contradiction to the fundamental law of dialectic reasoning. This law, indeed, by no means excludes, but, on the contrary, includes the idea that the systematic knowledge of the external universe can make giant strides from age to age.

The perception of the fundamental contradiction in German idealism led necessarily back to materialism, but *nota bene,* not to the simply metaphysical, exclusively mechanical materialism of the eighteenth century. Old materialism looked upon all previous history as a crude heap of irrationality and violence; modern materialism sees in it the process of evolution of humanity, and aims at discovering the laws thereof. With the French of the eighteenth century, and even with Hegel, the conception obtained of nature as a whole, moving in narrow circles, and forever immutable, with its eternal celestial bodies, as Newton, and unalterable organic species, as Linnæus, taught. Modern materialism embraces the more recent discoveries of natural science according to which nature also has its history in time, the celestial bodies, like the organic species that, under favourable conditions, people them, being born and perishing. And even if nature, as a whole, must still be said to move in recurrent cycles, these cycles assume infinitely larger dimensions. In both aspects, modern materialism is essentially dialectic, and no longer requires the assistance of that sort of philosophy which, queen-like, pretended to rule the remaining mob of sciences. As soon as each special science is bound to make clear its position in the great totality of things and of our knowledge of things, a special science dealing with this totality is superfluous or unnecessary. That which still survives of all earlier philosophy is the science of thought and its laws—formal logic and dialectics. Everything else is subsumed in the positive science of nature and history.

Whilst, however, the revolution in the conception of nature could only be made in proportion to the corresponding positive materials furnished by research, already much earlier certain historical facts had occurred which led to a decisive change in the conception of history. In 1831, the first working class rising took place in Lyons; between 1838 and 1842, the first national working class movement, that of the English Chartists, reached its height. The class struggle between proletariat and bourgeoisie came to the front in the history of the most ad-·· vanced countries in Europe, in proportion to the development, upon the one hand, of modern industry, upon the other, of the newly-acquired political supremacy of the bourgeoisie. Facts more and more strenuously gave the lie to the teachings of bourgeois economy as to the identity of the interests of capital and labour, as to the universal harmony and universal prosperity that would be the consequence of unbridled competition. All these things could no longer be ignored, any more than the French and English socialism, which was their theoretical, though very imperfect, expression. But the old idealist conception of history, which was not yet dislodged, knew nothing of class struggles based upon economic interests, knew nothing of economic interests; production and all economic relations appeared in it only as incidental, subordinate elements in the "history of civilisation."

The new facts made imperative a new examination of all past history. Then it was seen that *all* past history, with the exception of its primitive stages, was the history of class struggles; that these warring classes of society are always the products of the modes of production and of exchange—in a word, of the *economic* conditions of their time; that the economic structure of society always furnishes the real basis, starting from which we can alone work out the ultimate explanation of the whole superstructure of juridical and political institutions as well as of the religious, philosophical and other ideas of a given historical period. Hegel had freed history from metaphysics— he had made it dialectic; but his conception of history was es-

sentially idealistic. But now idealism was driven from its last
refuge, the philosophy of history; now a materialistic treatment
of history was propounded, and a method found of explaining
man's "knowing" by his "being," instead of, as heretofore, his
"being" by his "knowing."

From that time forward socialism was no longer an accidental
discovery of this or that ingenious brain, but the necessary outcome of the struggle between two historically developed classes—
the proletariat and the bourgeoisie. Its task was no longer to
manufacture a system of society as perfect as possible, but to
examine the historico-economic succession of events from which
these classes and their antagonisms had of necessity sprung,
and to discover in the economic conditions thus created the
means of ending the conflict. But the socialism of earlier days
was as incompatible with this materialistic conception as the
conception of nature of the French materialists was with dialectics and modern natural science. The socialism of earlier
days certainly criticised the existing capitalistic mode of production and its consequences. But it could not explain them,
and, therefore, could not get the mastery of them. It could
only simply reject them as bad. The more strongly this earlier
socialism denounced the exploitation of the working class, inevitable under capitalism, the less able was it clearly to show
in what this exploitation consisted and how it arose. But for
this it was necessary—1) to present the capitalistic method of
production in its historical connection and its inevitableness
during a particular historical period, and therefore, also, to
present its inevitable downfall; and 2) to lay bare its essential
character, which was still a secret. This was done by the
discovery of *surplus value*. It was shown that the appropriation of unpaid labour is the basis of the capitalist mode of
production and of the exploitation of the worker that occurs
under it; that even if the capitalist buys the labour power of
his labourer at its full value as a commodity on the market, he
yet extracts more value from it than he paid for; and that in
the ultimate analysis this surplus value forms those sums of
value from which are heaped up the constantly increasing masses
of capital in the hands of the possessing classes. The genesis

of capitalist production and the production of capital were both explained.

These two great discoveries, the materialistic conception of history and the revelation of the secret of capitalistic production through surplus value, we owe to Marx. With these discoveries socialism became a science. The next thing was to work out all its details and relations.

III

THE materialist conception of history starts from the proposition that the production of the means to support human life and, next to production, the exchange of things produced, is the basis of all social structure; that in every society that has appeared in history, the manner in which wealth is distributed and society divided into classes or orders is dependent upon what is produced, how it is produced, and how the products are exchanged. From this point of view the final causes of all social changes and political revolutions are to be sought, not in men's brains, not in man's better insight into eternal truth and justice, but in changes in the modes of production and exchange. They are to be sought, not in the *philosophy*, but in the *economics* of each particular epoch. The growing perception that existing social institutions are unreasonable and unjust, that reason has become unreason, and right wrong, is only proof that in the modes of production and exchange changes have silently taken place, with which the social order, adapted to earlier economic conditions, is no longer in keeping. From this it also follows that the means of getting rid of the incongruities that have been brought to light must also be present, in a more or less developed condition, within the changed modes of production themselves. These means are not to be invented by deduction from fundamental principles, but are to be discovered in the stubborn facts of the existing system of production.

What is, then, the position of modern socialism in this connection?

The present structure of society—this is now pretty generally conceded—is the creation of the ruling class of today, of the bourgeoisie. The mode of production peculiar to the bourgeoisie, known, since Marx, as the capitalist mode of production, was incompatible with the feudal system, with the privileges it conferred upon individuals, entire social ranks and local corporations, as well as with the hereditary ties of subordination which

54

constituted the framework of its social organization. The bourgeoisie broke up the feudal system and built upon its ruins the capitalist order of society, the kingdom of free competition, of personal liberty, of the equality, before the law, of all commodity owners, of all the rest of the capitalist blessings. Thenceforward the capitalist mode of production could develop in freedom. Since steam, machinery and the making of machines by machinery transformed the older manufacture into modern industry, the productive forces evolved under the guidance of the bourgeoisie developed with a rapidity and in a degree unheard of before. But just as the older manufacture, in its time, and handicraft, becoming more developed under its influence, had come into collision with the feudal trammels of the guilds, so now modern industry, in its more complete development, comes into collision with the bounds within which the capitalistic mode of production holds it confined. The new productive forces have already outgrown the capitalistic mode of using them. And this conflict between productive forces and modes of production is not a conflict engendered in the mind of man, like that between original sin and divine justice. It exists, in fact, objectively, outside us, independently of the will and actions even of the men that have brought it on. Modern socialism is nothing but the reflex, in thought, of this conflict in fact; its ideal reflection in the minds, first, of the class directly suffering under it, the working class.

Now, in what does this conflict consist?

Before capitalistic production, *i.e.*, in the Middle Ages, the system of petty industry obtained generally, based upon the private property of the labourers in their means of production; in the country, the agriculture of the small peasant, freeman or serf; in the towns, the handicrafts organised in guilds. The instruments of labour—land, agricultural implements, the workshop, the tool—were the instruments of labour of single individuals, adapted for the use of one worker, and, therefore, of necessity, small, dwarfish, circumscribed. But for this very reason they belonged, as a rule, to the producer himself. To concentrate these scattered, limited means of production, to enlarge them, to turn them into the powerful levers of production of the present day—this was precisely the historic rôle of capitalist production and of its upholder, the bourgeoisie. In the fourth section of *Capital* Marx has explained in detail, how since the fifteenth century this has been historically worked out through the three phases of simple co-operation, manufacture and modern industry. But the bourgeoisie, as is also shown there, could not transform these puny means of production into mighty productive forces, without transforming them, at the same time, from means of production of the individual into *social* means of production only workable by a collectivity of men. The spinning-wheel, the hand-loom, the blacksmith's hammer were replaced by the spinning machine, the power-loom, the steam-hammer; the individual workshop, by the factory, implying the co-operation of hundreds and thousands of workmen. In like manner, production itself changed from a series of individual into a series of social acts, and the products from individual to social products. The yarn, the cloth, the metal articles that now came out of the factory were the joint product of many workers, through whose hands they had successively to pass before they were ready. No one person could say of them: "I made that; this is *my* product."

But where, in a given society, the fundamental form of production is that spontaneous division of labour which creeps in gradually and not upon any preconceived plan, there the products take on the form of *commodities,* whose mutual exchange, buying and selling, enable the individual producers to satisfy their manifold wants. And this was the case in the Middle Ages. The peasant, *e.g.,* sold to the artisan agricultural products and bought from him the products of handicraft. Into this society of individual producers, of commodity producers, the new mode of production thrust itself. In the midst of the old division of labour, grown up spontaneously and upon *no definite plan,* which had governed the whole of society, now arose division of labour upon *a definite plan,* as organised in the factory; side by side with *individual* production appeared *social* production. The products of both were sold in the same market, and, therefore, at prices at least approximately equal. But organisation upon a definite plan was stronger than spontaneous division of labour. The factories working with the combined social forces of a collectivity of individuals produced their commodities far more cheaply than the individual small producers. Individual production succumbed in one department after another. Socialised production revolutionised all the old methods of production. But its revolutionary character was, at the same time, so little recognised, that it was, on the contrary, introduced as a means of increasing and developing the production of commodities. When it arose, it found ready-made, and made liberal use of, certain machinery for the production and exchange of commodities; merchants' capital, handicraft, wage labour. Socialised production thus introducing itself as a new form of the production of commodities, it was a matter of course that under it the old forms of appropriation remained in full swing, and were applied to its products as well.

In the mediæval stage of evolution of the production of commodities, the question as to the owner of the product of labour could not arise. The individual producer, as a rule, had, from raw material belonging to himself, and generally his own handiwork, produced it with his own tools, by the labour of his own hands or of his family. There was no need for him to appropriate the new product. It belonged wholly to him, as a matter of course. His property in the product was, therefore, based *upon his own labour*. Even where external help was used, this was, as a rule, of little importance, and very generally was compensated by something other than wages. The apprentices and journeymen of the guilds worked less for board and wages than for education, in order that they might become master craftsmen themselves.

Then came the concentration of the means of production and of the producers in large workshops and manufactories, their transformation into actual socialised means of production and socialised producers. But the socialised producers and means of production and their products were still treated, after this change, just as they had been before, *i.e.*, as the means of production and the products of individuals. Hitherto, the owner of the instruments of labour had himself appropriated the product, because as a rule it was his own product and the assistance of others was the exception. Now the owner of the instruments of labour always appropriated to himself the product, although it was no longer *his* product but exclusively the product of the *labour of others*. Thus, the products now produced socially were not appropriated by those who had actually set in motion the means of production and actually produced the commodities, but by the *capitalists*. The means of production, and production itself, had become in essence socialised. But they were subjected to a form of appropriation which presupposes the private production of individuals, under which, therefore, every one owns his own product and brings it to market. The mode of production is subjected to this form of appropriation, although it abolishes the conditions upon which the latter rests.*

This contradiction, which gives to the new mode of production its capitalistic character, *contains the germ of the whole of the social antagonisms of today*. The greater the mastery obtained by the new mode of production over all important fields of production and in all manufacturing countries, the more it reduced individual production to an insignificant residuum, *the more clearly was brought out the incompatibility of socialised production with capitalistic appropriation*.

The first capitalists found, as we have said, alongside of other forms of labour, wage labour ready-made for them on the market. But it was exceptional, complementary, necessary, transitory wage labour. The agricultural labourer, though, upon occasion, he hired himself out by the day, had a few acres of his own land on which he could at all events live at a pinch. The guilds were so organised that the journeyman of today became the master of tomorrow. But all this changed, as soon as the means of production became socialised and concentrated in the hands of capitalists. The means of production, as well as the product of the individual producer became more and more worthless; there was nothing left for him but to turn wage

---

*It is hardly necessary in this connection to point out, that, even if the form of appropriation remains the same, the *character* of the appropriation is just as much revolutionised as production is by the changes described above. It is, of course, a very different matter whether I appropriate to myself my own product or that of another. Note in passing that wage labour, which contains the whole capitalistic mode of production in embryo, is very ancient; in a sporadic, scattered form it existed for centuries alongside of slave labour. But the embryo could duly develop into the capitalistic mode of production only when the necessary historical pre-conditions had been furnished.

worker under the capitalist. Wage labour, aforetime the exception and accessory, now became the rule and basis of all production; aforetime complementary, it now became the sole remaining function of the worker. The wage worker for a time became a wage worker for life. The number of these permanent wage workers was further enormously increased by the breaking up of the feudal system that occurred at the same time, by the disbanding of the retainers of the feudal lords, the eviction of the peasants from their homesteads, etc. The separation was made complete between the means of production concentrated in the hands of the capitalists on the one side, and the producers, possessing nothing but their labour power, on the other. *The contradiction between socialised production and capitalistic appropriation manifested itself as the antagonism of proletariat and bourgeoisie.*

We have seen that the capitalistic mode of production thrust its way into a society of commodity producers, of individual producers, whose social bond was the exchange of their products. But every society, based upon the production of commodities, has this peculiarity: that the producers have lost control over their own social inter-relations. Each man produces for himself with such means of production as he may happen to have, and for such exchange as he may require to satisfy his remaining wants. No one knows how much of his particular article is coming on the market, nor how much of it will be wanted. No one knows whether his individual product will meet an actual demand, whether he will be able to make good his cost of production or even to sell his commodity at all. Anarchy reigns in socialised production.

But the production of commodities, like every other form of production, has its peculiar inherent laws inseparable from it; and these laws work, despite anarchy, in and through anarchy. They reveal themselves in the only persistent form of social inter-relations, *i.e.*, in exchange, and here they affect the individual producers as compulsory laws of competition. They are, at first, unknown to these producers themselves, and have to be discovered by them gradually and as the result of experience. They work themselves out, therefore, independently of the producers, and in antagonism to them, as inexorable natural laws of their particular form of production. The product governs the producers.

In mediæval society, especially in the earlier centuries, production was essentially directed towards satisfying the wants of the individual. It satisfied, in the main, only the wants of the producer and his family. Where relations of personal dependence existed, as in the country, it also helped to satisfy the wants of the feudal lord. In all this there was, therefore, no exchange; the products, consequently, did not assume the character of commodities. The family of the peasant produced almost everything they wanted: clothes and furniture, as well as means of subsistence. Only when it began to produce more than was sufficient to supply its own wants and the payments in kind to the feudal lord, only then did it also produce commodities. This surplus, thrown into socialised exchange and offered for sale, became commodities.

The artisans of the towns, it is true, had from the first to produce for exchange. But they, also, themselves supplied the greatest part of their own individual wants. They had gardens and plots of land. They turned their cattle out into the communal forest, which, also, yielded them timber and firing. The women spun flax, wool, and so forth. Production for the purpose of exchange, production of commodities was only in its infancy. Hence, exchange was restricted, the market narrow, the methods of production stable; there was local exclusiveness without, local unity within; the mark * in the country, in the town, the guild.

But with the extension of the production of commodities, and especially with the introduction of the capitalist mode of production, the laws of commodity production, hitherto latent, came into action more openly and with greater force. The old bonds were loosened, the old exclusive limits broken through, the producers were more and more turned into independent, isolated producers of commodities. It became apparent that the production of society at large was ruled by absence of plan, by accident, by anarchy; and this anarchy grew to greater and greater height. But the chief means by aid of which the capitalist mode of production intensified this anarchy of

* See Appendix.—*Ed.*

socialised production was the exact opposite of anarchy. It was the increasing organisation of production, upon a social basis, in every individual productive establishment. By this, the old, peaceful, stable condition of things was ended. Wherever this organisation of production was introduced into a branch of industry, it brooked no other method of production by its side. The field of labour became a battle ground. The great geographical discoveries, and the colonisation following upon them, multiplied markets and quickened the transformation of handicraft into manufacture. The war did not simply break out between the individual producers of particular localities. The local struggles begat in their turn national conflicts, the commercial wars of the seventeenth and the eighteenth centuries.

Finally, modern industry and the opening of the world market made the struggle universal, and at the same time gave it an unheard-of virulence. Advantages in natural or artificial conditions of production now decide the existence or non-existence of individual capitalists, as well as of whole industries and countries. He that falls is remorsely cast aside. It is the Darwinian struggle of the individual for existence transferred from nature to society with intensified violence. The conditions of existence natural to the animal appear as the final term of human development. The contradiction between socialised production and capitalistic appropriation now presents itself as *an antagonism between the organisation of production in the individual workshop and the anarchy of production in society generally.*

The capitalistic mode of production moves in these two forms of the antagonism immanent to it from its very origin. It is never able to get out of that "vicious circle," which Fourier had already discovered. What Fourier could not, indeed, see in his time is: that this circle is gradually narrowing; that the movement becomes more and more a spiral, and must come to an end, like the movement of the planets, by collision with the centre. It is the compelling force of anarchy in the production of society at large that more and more completely turns the great majority of men into proletarians; and it is the masses of the proletariat again who will finally put an end to anarchy in production. It is the compelling force of anarchy in social production that turns the limitless perfectibility of machinery under modern industry into a compulsory law by which every individual industrial capitalist must perfect his machinery more and more, under penalty of ruin.

But the perfecting of machinery is making human labour superfluous. If the introduction and increase of machinery means the displacement of millions of manual, by a few machine workers, improvement in machinery means the displacement of more and more of the machine workers themselves. It means, in the last instance, the production of a number of available wage workers in excess of the average needs of capital, the formation of a complete industrial reserve army, as I called it in 1845,* available at the times when industry is working at high pressure, to be cast out upon the street when the inevitable crash comes, a constant dead weight upon the limbs of the working class in its struggle for existence with capital, a regulator for the keeping of wages down to the low level that suits the interests of capital. Thus it comes about, to quote Marx, that machinery becomes the most powerful weapon in the war of capital against the working class; that the instruments of labour constantly tear the means of subsistence out of the hands of the labourer; that the very product of the worker is turned into an instrument for his subjugation. Thus it comes about that the economising of the instruments of labour becomes at the same time, from the outset, the most reckless waste of labour power, and robbery based upon the normal conditions under which labour functions; that machinery, "the most powerful instrument for shortening labour time, becomes the most unfailing means for placing every moment of the labourer's time and that of his family at the disposal of the capitalist for the purpose of expanding the value of his capital." (*Capital,* English edition, p. 406.) Thus it comes about that overwork of some becomes the preliminary condition for the idleness of others, and that modern industry, which hunts after new consumers over the whole world, forces the consumption of the masses at home down to a starvation minimum, and in doing

* *The Condition of the Working Class in England,* Sonnenschein and Co., p. 84.

thus destroys its own home market. "The law that always equilibrates the relative surplus population, or industrial reserve army, to the extent and energy of accumulation, this law rivets the labourer to capital more firmly than the wedges of Vulcan did Prometheus to the rock. It establishes an accumulation of misery, corresponding with accumulation of capital. Accumulation of wealth at one pole is, therefore, at the same time, accumulation of misery, agony of toil, slavery, ignorance, brutality, mental degradation, at the opposite pole, *i.e.*, on the side of the class that produces *its own product in the form of capital.*" (Marx, *Capital,* Sonnenschein and Co., p. 661.) And to expect any other division of the products from the capitalistic mode of production is the same as expecting the electrodes of a battery not to decompose acidulated water, not to liberate oxygen at the positive, hydrogen at the negative pole, so long as they are connected with the battery.

We have seen that the ever-increasing perfectibility of modern machinery is, by the anarchy of social production, turned into a compulsory law that forces the individual industrial capitalist always to improve his machinery, always to increase its productive force. The bare possibility of extending the field of production is transformed for him into a similar compulsory law. The enormous expansive force of modern industry, compared with which that of gases is mere child's play, appears to us now as a *necessity* for expansion, both qualitative and quantitative, that laughs at all resistance. Such resistance is offered by consumption, by sales, by the markets for the products of modern industry. But the capacity for extension, extensive and intensive, of the markets is primarily governed by quite different laws, that work much less energetically. The extension of the markets cannot keep pace with the extension of production. The collision becomes inevitable, and as this cannot produce any real solution so long as it does not break in pieces the capitalist mode of production, the collisions become periodic. Capitalist production has begotten another "vicious circle."

As a matter of fact, since 1825, when the first general crisis broke out, the whole industrial and commercial world, production and exchange among all civilised peoples and their more or less barbaric hangers-on, are thrown out of joint about once every ten years. Commerce is at a standstill, the markets are glutted, products accumulate, as multitudinous as they are unsaleable, hard cash disappears, credit vanishes, factories are closed, the mass of the workers are in want of the means of subsistence, because they have produced too much of the means of subsistence; bankruptcy follows upon bankruptcy, execution upon execution. The stagnation lasts for years; productive forces and products are wasted and destroyed wholesale, until the accumulated mass of commodities finally filter off, more or less depreciated in value, until production and exchange gradually begin to move again. Little by little the pace quickens. It becomes a trot. The industrial trot breaks into a canter, the canter in turn grows into the headlong gallop of a perfect steeplechase of industry, commercial credit and speculation, which finally, after breakneck leaps, ends where it began—in the ditch of a crisis. And so over and over again. We have now, since the year 1825, gone through this five times, and at the present moment (1877) we are going through it for the sixth time. And the character of these crises is so clearly defined that Fourier hit all of them off when he described the first as *"crise pléthorique,"* a crisis from plethora.

In these crises, the contradiction between socialised production and capitalist appropriation ends in a violent explosion. The circulation of commodities is, for the time being, stopped. Money, the means of circulation, becomes a hindrance to circulation. All the laws of production and circulation of commodities are turned upside down. The economic collision has reached its apogee. *The mode of production is in rebellion against the mode of exchange.*

The fact that the socialised organisation of production within the factory has developed so far that it has become incompatible with the anarchy of production in society, which exists side by side with and dominates it, is brought home to the capitalists themselves by the violent concentration of capital that occurs during crises, through the ruin of many large, and a still greater number of small, capitalists. The whole mechanism of the capitalist mode of production breaks down under the pressure of the productive forces, its own creations. It is no longer able to turn all this mass of means of production into capital.

They lie fallow, and for that very reason the industrial reserve army must also lie fallow. Means of production, means of subsistence, available labourers, all the elements of production and of general wealth, are present in abundance. But "abundance becomes the source of distress and want" (Fourier), because it is the very thing that prevents the transformation of the means of production and subsistence into capital. For in capitalistic society the means of production can only function when they have undergone a preliminary transformation into capital, into the means of exploiting human labour power. The necessity of this transformation into capital of the means of production and subsistence stands like a ghost between these and the workers. It alone prevents the coming together of the material and personal levers of production; it alone forbids the means of production to function, the workers to work and live. On the one hand, therefore, the capitalistic mode of production stands convicted of its own incapacity to further direct these productive forces. On the other, these productive forces themselves, with increasing energy, press forward to the removal of the existing contradiction, to the abolition of their quality as capital, to the *practical recognition of their character as social productive forces.*

This rebellion of the productive forces, as they grow more and more powerful, against their quality as capital, this stronger and stronger command that their social character shall be recognised, forces the capitalist class itself to treat them more and more as social productive forces, so far as this is possible under capitalist conditions. The period of industrial high pressure, with its unbounded inflation of credit, not less than the crash itself, by the collapse of great capitalist establishments, tends to bring about that form of the socialisation of great masses of means of production, which we meet with in the different kinds of joint-stock companies. Many of these means of production and of distribution are, from the outset, so colossal, that, like the railroads, they exclude all other forms of capitalistic exploitation. At a further stage of evolution this form also becomes insufficient. The producers on a large scale in a particular branch of industry in a particular country unite in a "trust," a union for the purpose of regulating production.

They determine the total amount to be produced, parcel it out among themselves, and thus enforce the selling price fixed beforehand. But trusts of this kind, as soon as business becomes bad, are generally liable to break up, and, on this very account, compel a yet greater concentration of association. The whole of the particular industry is turned into one gigantic joint-stock company; internal competition gives place to the internal monopoly of this one company. This has happened in 1890 with the English *alkali* production, which is now, after the fusion of 48 large works, in the hands of one company, conducted upon a single plan, and with a capital of £6,000,000.

In the trusts, freedom of competition changes into its very opposite—into monopoly; and the production without any definite plan of capitalistic society capitulates to the production upon a definite plan of the invading socialistic society. Certainly this is so far still to the benefit and advantage of the capitalists. But in this case the exploitation is so palpable that it must break down. No nation will put up with production conducted by trusts, with so barefaced an exploitation of the community by a small band of dividend mongers.

In any case, with trusts or without, the official representative of capitalist society—the state—will ultimately have to undertake the direction of production.* This necessity of conversion

* I say "have to." For only when the means of production and distribution have *actually* outgrown the form of management by joint-stock companies, and when, therefore, the taking them over by the state has become *economically* inevitable, only then—even if it is the state of today that effects this—is there an economic advance, the attainment of another step preliminary to the taking over of all productive forces by society itself. But of late, since Bismarck went in for state ownership of industrial establishments, a kind of spurious socialism has arisen, degenerating, now and again, into something of flunkeyism, that without more ado declares *all* state ownership, even of the Bismarckian sort, to be socialistic. Certainly, if the taking over by the state of the tobacco industry is socialistic, then Napoleon and Metternich must be numbered among the founders of socialism. If the Belgian state, for quite ordinary political and financial reasons, itself constructed its chief railway lines; if Bismarck, not under any economic compulsion, took over for the state the chief Prussian lines, simply to be the better able to have them in hand in case of war, to bring up the railway employees as voting cattle for the government, and especially to create for himself a new source of income independent of parliamentary votes—this was, in no sense, a

into state property is felt first in the great institutions for intercourse and communication—the post-office, the telegraphs, the railways.

If the crises demonstrate the incapacity of the bourgeoisie for managing any longer modern productive forces, the transformation of the great establishments for production and distribution into joint-stock companies, trusts and state property, show how unnecessary the bourgeoisie are for that purpose. All the social functions of the capitalist are now performed by salaried employees. The capitalist has no further social function than that of pocketing dividends, tearing off coupons, and gambling on the Stock Exchange, where the different capitalists despoil one another of their capital. At first the capitalistic mode of production forces out the workers. Now it forces out the capitalists, and reduces them, just as it reduced the workers, to the ranks of the surplus population, although not immediately into those of the industrial reserve army.

But the transformation, either into joint-stock companies and trusts, or into state ownership, does not do away with the capitalistic nature of the productive forces. In the joint-stock companies and trusts this is obvious. And the modern state, again, is only the organisation that bourgeois society takes on in order to support the external conditions of the capitalist mode of production against the encroachments, as well of the workers as of individual capitalists. The modern state, no matter what its form, is essentially a capitalist machine, the state of the capitalists, the ideal personification of the total national capital. The more it proceeds to the taking over of productive forces, the more does it actually become the national capitalist, the more citizens does it exploit. The workers remain wage workers—proletarians. The capitalist relation is not done away with. It is rather brought to a head. But, brought to a head, it topples over. State ownership of the productive forces is not the solution of the conflict, but con-

socialistic measure, directly or indirectly, consciously or unconsciously. Otherwise, the Royal Maritime Company, the Royal porcelain manufacture, and even the regimental tailor of the army would also be socialistic institutions, or even, as was seriously proposed by a sly dog in Frederick William III's reign, the taking over by the state of the brothels.

cealed within it are the technical conditions that form the elements of that solution.

This solution can only consist in the practical recognition of the social nature of the modern forces of production, and therefore in the harmonising of the modes of production, appropriation and exchange with the socialised character of the means of production. And this can only come about by society openly and directly taking possession of the productive forces which have outgrown all control except that of society as a whole. The social character of the means of production and of the products today reacts against the producers, periodically disrupts all production and exchange, acts only like a law of nature working blindly, forcibly, destructively. But with the taking over by society of the productive forces, the social character of the means of production and of the products will be utilised by the producers with a perfect understanding of its nature, and instead of being a source of disturbance and periodical collapse, will become the most powerful lever of production itself.

Active social forces work exactly like natural forces; blindly, forcibly, destructively, so long as we do not understand and reckon with them. But when once we understand them, when once we grasp their action, their direction, their effects, it depends only upon ourselves to subject them more and more to our own will, and by means of them to reach our own ends. And this holds quite especially of the mighty productive forces of today. As long as we obstinately refuse to understand the nature and the character of these social means of action—and this understanding goes against the grain of the capitalist mode of production and its defenders—so long these forces are at work in spite of us, in opposition to us, so long they master us, as we have shown above in detail.

But when once their nature is understood, they can, in the hands of the producers working together, be transformed from master demons into willing servants. The difference is as that between the destructive force of electricity in the lightning of the storm, and electricity under command in the telegraph and the voltaic arc; the difference between a conflagration, and fire working in the service of man. With this recognition at last of the real nature of the productive forces of today, the social anarchy of production gives place to a social regulation of production upon a definite plan, according to the needs of the community and of each individual. Then the capitalist mode of appropriation, in which the product enslaves first the producer and then the appropriator, is replaced by the mode of appropriation of the products that is based upon the nature of the modern means of production; upon the one hand, direct social appropriation, as means to the maintenance and extension of production—on the other, direct individual appropriation, as means of subsistence and of enjoyment.

Whilst the capitalist mode of production more and more completely transforms the great majority of the population into proletarians, it creates the power which, under penalty of its own destruction, is forced to accomplish this revolution. Whilst it forces on more and more the transformation of the vast means of production, already socialised, into state property, it shows itself the way to accomplishing this revolution. *The proletariat seizes political power and turns the means of production into state property.*

But, in doing this, it abolishes itself as proletariat, abolishes all class distinctions and class antagonisms, abolishes also the state as state. Society thus far, based upon class antagonisms, had need of the state. That is, of an organisation of the particular class which was *pro tempore* the exploiting class, an organisation for the purpose of preventing any interference from without with the existing conditions of production, and therefore, especially, for the purpose of forcibly keeping the exploited classes in the condition of oppression corresponding with the given mode of production (slavery, serfdom, wage labour). The state was the official representative of society as a whole; the gathering of it together into a visible embodiment. But it was this only in so far as it was the state of that class which itself represented, for the time being, society as a whole; in ancient times, the state of slave-owning citizens; in the Middle Ages, the feudal lords; in our own time, the bourgeoisie. When at last it becomes the real representative of the whole of society, it renders itself unnecessary. As soon as there is no longer any social class to be held in subjection; as soon as class rule and the individual struggle for existence based upon our present anarchy in production, with the collisions and excesses arising from these, are removed, nothing more remains to be repressed, and a special repressive force, a state, is no longer necessary. The first act by virtue of which the state really constitutes itself the representative of the whole of society—the taking possession of the means of production in the name of society—this is, at the same time, its last independent act as a state. State interference in social relations becomes, in one domain after another, superfluous, and then dies out of itself; the government of persons is replaced by the administration of things, and by the conduct of processes of production. The state is not "abolished." *It dies out.* This gives the measure of the value of the phrase "a free state," both as to its justifiable use at times by agitators, and as to its ultimate scientific insufficiency; and also of the demands of the so-called anarchists for the abolition of the state out of hand.

Since the historical appearance of the capitalist mode of production, the appropriation by society of all the means of production has often been dreamed of, more or less vaguely, by individuals, as well as by sects, as the ideal of the future. But it could become possible, could become a historical necessity, only when the actual conditions for its realisation were there. Like every other social advance, it becomes practicable, not by men understanding that the existence of classes is in contradiction to justice, equality, etc., not by the mere willingness to abolish these classes, but by virtue of certain new economic conditions. The separation of society into an exploiting and an exploited class, a ruling and an oppressed class, was the necessary consequence of the deficient and restricted development of production in former times. So long as the total social labour only yields a produce which but slightly exceeds that barely necessary for the existence of all; so long, therefore, as labour engages all or almost all the time of the great majority of the members of society—so long, of necessity, this society is divided into classes. Side by side with the great majority, exclusively bond slaves to labour, arises a class freed from directly productive labour, which looks after the general affairs of society, the direction of labour, state business, law, science, art, etc. It is, therefore, the law of division of labour that lies at the basis of the division into classes. But this does not prevent this division into classes from being carried out by means of violence and robbery, trickery and fraud. It does not prevent the ruling class, once having the upper hand, from consolidating its power at the expense of the working class, from turning their social leadership into an intensified exploitation of the masses.

But if, upon this showing, division into classes has a certain historical justification, it has this only for a given period, only under given social conditions. It was based upon the insufficiency of production. It will be swept away by the complete development of modern productive forces. And, in fact, the abolition of classes in society presupposes a degree of historical evolution, at which the existence, not simply of this or that particular ruling class, but of any ruling class at all, and, therefore, the existence of class distinction itself has become an obsolete anachronism. It presupposes, therefore, the development of production carried out to a degree at which appropriation of the means of production and of the products, and, with this, of political domination, of the monopoly of culture, and of intellectual leadership by a particular class of society, has become not only superfluous, but economically, politically, intellectually a hindrance to development.

This point is now reached. Their political and intellectual bankruptcy is scarcely any longer a secret to the bourgeoisie themselves. Their economic bankruptcy recurs regularly every ten years. In every crisis, society is suffocated beneath the weight of its own productive forces and products, which it cannot use, and stands helpless, face to face with the absurd contradiction that the producers have nothing to consume, because consumers are wanting. The expansive force of the means of production bursts the bonds that the capitalist mode of production had imposed upon them. Their deliverance from these bonds is the one precondition for an unbroken, constantly accelerated development of the productive forces, and therewith for a practically unlimited increase of production itself. Nor is this all. The socialised appropriation of the means of production does away not only with the present artificial restrictions upon production, but also with the positive waste and devastation of productive forces and products that are at the present time the inevitable concomitants of production, and that reach their height in the crises. Further, it sets free for the community at large a mass of means of production and of products, by doing away with the senseless extravagance of the ruling classes of today, and their political representatives. The possibility of securing for every member of society, by means of socialised production, an existence not only fully sufficient materially, and becoming day by day more full, but an existence guaranteeing to all the free development and exercise of their physical and mental faculties—this possibility is now for the first time here, but *it is here.**

With the seizing of the means of production by society, production of commodities is done away with, and, simultaneously, the mastery of the product over the producer. Anarchy in social production is replaced by systematic definite organisation. The struggle for individual existence disappears. Then for the first time, man, in a certain sense, is finally marked off from the rest of the animal kingdom, and emerges from mere animal conditions of existence into really human ones. The whole sphere of the conditions of life which environ man, and which have hitherto ruled man, now comes under the dominion and control of man, who for the first time becomes the real, conscious lord of nature, because he has now become master of his own social organisation. The laws of his own social action, hitherto standing face to face with man as laws of nature foreign to and dominating him, will then be used with full understanding, and so mastered by him. Man's own social organisation, hitherto confronting him as a necessity imposed by

* A few figures may serve to give an approximate idea of the enormous expansive force of the modern means of production, even under capitalist pressure. According to Mr. Giffen, the total wealth of Great Britain and Ireland amounted, in round numbers, in

1814 to £2,200,000,000
1865 to £6,100,000,000
1875 to £8,500,000,000

As an instance of the squandering of means of production and of products during a crisis, the total loss in the Germany iron industry alone, in the crisis 1873-78, was given at the second German Industrial Congress (Berlin, February 21, 1878) as £22,750,000.

nature and history, now becomes the result of his own free action. The extraneous objective forces that have hitherto governed history pass under the control of man himself. Only from that time will man himself, more and more consciously, make his own history—only from that time will the social causes set in movement by him have, in the main and in a constantly growing measure, the results intended by him. It is the ascent of man from the kingdom of necessity to the kingdom of freedom.

Let us briefly sum up our sketch of historical evolution.

I. *Mediæval Society*—Individual production on a small scale. Means of production adapted for individual use; hence primitive, ungainly, petty, dwarfed in action. Production for immediate consumption, either of the producer himself or of his feudal lords. Only where an excess of production over this consumption occurs is such excess offered for sale, enters into exchange. Production of commodities, therefore, is only in its infancy. But already it contains within itself, in embryo, *anarchy in the production of society at large.*

II. *Capitalist Revolution*—Transformation of industry, at first by means of simple co-operation and manufacture. Concentration of the means of production, hitherto scattered, into great workshops. As a consequence, their transformation from individual to social means of production—a transformation which does not, on the whole, affect the form of exchange. The old forms of appropriation remain in force. The capitalist appears. In his capacity as owner of the means of production, he also appropriates the products and turns them into commodities. Production has become a *social* act. Exchange and appropriation continue to be *individual* acts, the acts of individuals. *The social product is appropriated by the individual capitalist.* Fundamental contradiction, whence arise all the contradictions in which our present day society moves, and which modern industry brings to light.

A. Severance of the producer from the means of production. Condemnation of the worker to wage labour for life. *Antagonism between the proletariat and the bourgeoisie.*

B. Growing predominance and increasing effectiveness of the laws governing the production of commodities. Unbridled competition. *Contradiction between socialised organisation in the individual factory and social anarchy in production as a whole.*

C. On the one hand, perfecting of machinery, made by competition compulsory for each individual manufacturer, and complemented by a constantly growing displacement of labourers. *Industrial reserve army.* On the other hand, unlimited extension of production, also compulsory under competition, for every manufacturer. On both sides, unheard of development of productive forces, excess of supply over demand, overproduction, glutting of the markets, crises every ten years, the vicious circle: excess here, of means of production and products—excess there, of labourers, without employment and without means of existence. But these two levers of production and of social wellbeing are unable to work together because the capitalist form of production prevents the productive forces from working and the products from circulating, unless they are first turned into capital—which their very superabundance prevents. The contradiction has grown into an absurdity. *The mode of production rises in rebellion against the form of exchange.* The bourgeoisie are convicted of incapacity further to manage their own social productive forces.

D. Partial recognition of the social character of the productive forces forced upon the capitalists themselves. Taking over of the great institutions for production and communication, first by joint-stock companies, later on by trusts, then by the state. The bourgeoisie demonstrated to be a superfluous class. All its social functions are now performed by salaried employees.

III. *Proletarian Revolution*—Solution of the contradictions. The proletariat seizes the public power, and by means of this transforms the socialised means of production, slipping from the hands of the bourgeoisie, into public property. By this act, the proletariat frees the means of production from the character of capital they have thus far borne, and gives their socialised character complete freedom to work itself out. Socialised production upon a predetermined plan becomes henceforth possible. The development of production makes the existence of different classes of society thenceforth an anachronism. In proportion as anarchy in social production vanishes, the political authority of the state dies out. Man, at last the master of his own form of social organisation, becomes at the same time the lord over nature, his own master—free.

To accomplish this act of universal emancipation is the historical mission of the modern proletariat. To thoroughly comprehend the historical conditions and thus the very nature of this act, to impart to the now oppressed proletarian class a full knowledge of the conditions and of the meaning of the momentous act it is called upon to accomplish, this is the task of the theoretical expression of the proletarian movement, scientific socialism.

APPENDIX

THE MARK *

In a country like Germany, in which quite half the population live by agriculture, it is necessary that the socialist workingmen, and through them the peasants, should learn how the present system of landed property, large as well as small, has arisen. It is necessary to contrast the misery of the agricultural labourers of the present time and the mortgage servitude of the small peasants, with the old common property of all free men in what was then in truth their "fatherland," the free common possession of all by inheritance.

I shall give, therefore, a short historical sketch of the primitive agrarian conditions of the German tribes. A few traces of these have survived until our own time, but all through the Middle Ages they served as the basis and as the type of all public institutions, and permeated the whole of public life, not only in Germany, but also in the north of France, England and Scandinavia. And yet they have been so completely forgotten, that recently G. L. Maurer has had to rediscover their real significance.

Two fundamental facts, that arose spontaneously, govern the primitive history of all, or of almost all, nations; the grouping of the people according to kindred and common property in the soil. And this was the case with the Germans. As they had brought with them from Asia the method of grouping by tribes and gentes, as they even in the time of the Romans so drew up their battle array, that those related to each other always stood shoulder to shoulder, this grouping also governed the partitioning of their new territory east of the Rhine and north of the Danube. Each tribe settled down upon the new possession, not according to whim or accident, but, as Cæsar ex-

* See p. 60.—*Ed.*

pressly states, according to the gens relationship between the members of the tribe. A particular area was apportioned to each of the nearly related larger groups, and on this again the individual gentes, each including a certain number of families, settled down by villages. A number of allied villages formed a hundred (old high German, *huntari;* old Norse, *heradh*). A number of hundreds formed a *gau* or shire. The sum total of the shires was the people itself.

The land which was not taken possession of by the village remained at the disposal of the hundred. What was not assigned to the latter remained for the shire. Whatever after that was still to be disposed of—generally a very large tract of land—was the immediate possession of the whole people. Thus in Sweden we find all these different stages of common holding side by side. Each village had its village common land (*bys almänningar*), and beyond this was the hundred common land (*härads*), the shire common lands (*lands*), and finally the people's common land. This last, claimed by the king as representative of the whole nation, was known therefore as *Konungs almänningar.* But all of these, even the royal lands, were named, without distinction, *almänningar,* common land.

This old Swedish arrangement of the common land, in its minute subdivision, evidently belongs to a later stage of development. If it ever did exist in Germany, it soon vanished. The rapid increase in the population led to the establishment of a number of daughter villages on the *mark, i.e.,* on the large tract of land attributed to each individual mother village. These daughter villages formed a single mark association with the mother village, on the basis of equal or of restricted rights. Thus we find everywhere in Germany, so far as research goes back, a larger or smaller number of villages united in one mark association. But these associations were, at least, at first, still subject to the great federations of the marks of the hundred, or of the shire. And, finally, the people, as a whole, originally formed one single great mark association, not only for the administration of the land that remained the immediate possession of the people, but also as a supreme court over the subordinate local marks.

Until the time when the Frankish kingdom subdued Germany

east of the Rhine, the centre of gravity of the mark association
seems to have been in the *gau* or shire—the shire seems to have
formed the unit mark association. For, upon this assumption
alone is it explicable that, upon the official division of the
kingdom, so many old and large marks reappear as shires. Soon
after this time began the decay of the old large marks. Yet
even in the code known as the *Kaiserrecht*, the "Emperor's Law"
of the thirteenth or fourteenth century, it is a general rule that
a mark includes from six to twelve villages.

In Cæsar's time a great part at least of the Germans, the
Suevi, to wit, who had not yet got any fixed settlement, cultivated their fields in common. From analogy with other peoples
we may take it that this was carried on in such a way that the
individual gentes, each including a number of nearly related
families, cultivated in common the land apportioned to them,
which was changed from year to year, and divided the products
among the families. But after the Suevi, about the beginning
of our era, had settled down in their new domains, this soon
ceased. At all events, Tacitus (150 years after Cæsar) only
mentions the tilling of the soil by individual families. But the
land to be tilled only belonged to these for a year. Every year
it was divided up anew and redistributed.

How this was done, is still to be seen at the present
time on the Moselle and in the Hochwald, on the so-called
"*Gehöferschaften.*" There the whole of the land under cultivation, arable and meadows, not annually it is true, but every three,
six, nine, or twelve years, is thrown together and parcelled out
into a number of "*Gewanne,*" or areas, according to situation
and the quality of the soil. Each *Gewann* is again divided into
as many equal parts, long, narrow strips, as there are claimants
in the association. These are shared by lot among the members,
so that every member receives an equal portion in each *Gewann*.
At the present time the shares have become unequal by divisions
among heirs, sales, etc.; but the old full share still furnishes the
unit that determines the half, or quarter, or one-eighth shares.
The uncultivated land, forest and pasture land, is still a common
possession for common use.

The same primitive arrangement obtained until the beginning
of this century in the so-called assignments by lot (*Loosgüter*)

of the Rhein palatinate in Bavaria, whose arable land has since been turned into the private property of individuals. The *Gehöferschaften* also find it more and more to their interest to let the periodical re-division become obsolete and to turn the changing ownership into settled private property. Thus most of them, if not all, have died out in the last forty years and given place to villages with peasant proprietors using the forests and pasture land in common.

The first piece of ground that passed into the private property of individuals was that on which the house stood. The inviolability of the dwelling, that basis of all personal freedom, was transferred from the caravan of the nomadic train to the log house of the stationary peasant, and gradually was transformed into a complete right of property in the homestead. This had already come about in the time of Tacitus. The free German's homestead must, even in that time, have been excluded from the mark, and thereby inaccessible to its officials, a safe place of refuge for fugitives, as we find it described in the regulations of the marks of later times, and to some extent, even in the *"leges Barbarorum,"* the codifications of German tribal customary law, written down from the fifth to the eighth century. For the sacredness of the dwelling was not the effect but the cause of its transformation into private property.

Four or five hundred years after Tacitus, according to the same law books, the cultivated land also was the hereditary, although not the absolute freehold property of individual peasants, who had the right to dispose of it by sale or any other means of transfer. The causes of this transformation, as far as we can trace them, are twofold.

First, from the beginning there were in Germany itself, besides the close villages already described, with their complete ownership in common of the land, other villages where, besides homesteads, the fields also were excluded from the mark, the property of the community, and were parcelled out among the individual peasants as their hereditary property. But this was only the case where the nature of the place, so to say, compelled it: in narrow valleys, and on narrow, flat ridges between marshes, as in Westphalia; later on, in the Odenwald, and in almost all the Alpine valleys. In these places the village consisted, as it does now, of scattered individual dwellings, each surrounded by the fields belonging to it. A periodical re-division of the arable land was in these cases hardly possible, and so what remained within the mark was only the circumjacent untilled land. When, later, the right to dispose of the homestead by transfer to a third person became an important consideration, those who were free owners of their fields found themselves in an advantageous position. The wish to attain these advantages may have led in many of the villages with common ownership of the land to the letting the customary method of partition die out and to the transformation of the individual shares of the members into hereditary and transferable freehold property.

But, second, conquest led the Germans on to Roman territory, where, for centuries, the soil had been private property (the unlimited property of Roman law), and where the small number of conquerors could not possibly altogether do away with a form of holding so deeply rooted. The connection of hereditary private property in fields and meadows with Roman law, at all events on territory that had been Roman, is supported by the fact that such remains of common property in arable land as have come down to our time are found on the left bank of the Rhine—*i.e.*, on conquered territory, but territory *thoroughly Germanised*. When the Franks settled here in the fifth century, common ownership in the fields must still have existed among them, otherwise we should not find there *Gehöferschaften* and *Loosgüter*. But here also private ownership soon got the mastery, for this form of holding only do we find mentioned, in so far as arable land is concerned, in the Riparian law of the sixth century. And in the interior of Germany, as I have said, the cultivated land also soon became private property.

But if the German conquerors adopted private ownership in fields and meadows—*i.e.*, gave up at the first division of the land, or soon after, any repartition (for it was nothing more than this), they introduced, on the other hand, everywhere their German mark system, with common holding of woods and pastures, together with the over-lordship of the mark in respect to the partitioned land. This happened not only with the Franks in the north of France and the Anglo-Saxons in England, but also with the Burgundians in Eastern France, the Visigoths in

the south of France and Spain, and the Ostrogoths and Lango-
bardians in Italy. In these last-named countries, however, as
far as is known, traces of the mark government have lasted
until the present time almost exclusively in the higher mountain
regions.

The form that the mark government has assumed after the
periodical partition of the cultivated land had fallen into disuse
is that which now meets us, not only in the old popular laws
of the fifth, sixth, seventh and eighth centuries, but also in the
English and Scandinavian law books of the Middle Ages, in the
many German mark regulations (the so-called *Weisthümer*)
from the fifteenth to the seventeenth century, and in the customary laws (*coûtumes*) of Northern France.

Whilst the association of the mark gave up the right of, from
time to time, partitioning fields and meadows anew among its
individual members, it did not give up a single one of its other
rights over these lands. And these rights were very important.
The association had only transferred their fields to individuals
with a view to their being used as arable and meadow land, and
with that view alone. Beyond that the individual owner had no
right. Treasures found in the earth, if they lay deeper than
the ploughshare goes, did not, therefore, originally belong to
him, but to the community. It was the same thing with digging
for ores, and the like. All these rights were, later on, stolen
by the princes and landlords for their own use.

But, further, the use of arable and meadow lands was under
the supervision and direction of the community and that in the
following form. Wherever three-field farming obtained—and
that was almost everywhere—the whole cultivated area of the
village was divided into three equal parts, each of which was
alternately sown one year with winter seed, the second with
summer seed, and the third lay fallow. Thus the village had
each year its winter field, its summer field, its fallow field. In
the partition of the land care was taken that each member's
share was made up of equal portions from each of the three
fields, so that everyone could, without difficulty, accommodate
himself to the regulations of the community, in accordance with
which he would have to sow autumn seed only in his winter
field, and so on.

The field whose turn it was to lie fallow returned, for the time being, into the common possession, and served the community in general for pasture. And as soon as the two other fields were reaped, they likewise became again common property until seed time, and were used as common pasturage. The same thing occurred with the meadows after the aftermath. The owners had to remove the fences upon all fields given over to pasturage. This compulsory pasturage, of course, made it necessary that the time of sowing and of reaping should not be left to the individual, but be fixed for all by the community or by custom.

All other land, *i.e.*, all that was not house and farmyard, or so much of the mark as had been distributed among individuals, remained, as in early times, common property for common use; forests, pasture lands, heaths, moors, rivers, ponds, lakes, roads and bridges, hunting and fishing grounds. Just as the share of each member in so much of the mark as was distributed was of equal size, so was his share also in the use of the "common mark." The nature of this use was determined by the members of the community as a whole. So, too, was the mode of partition, if the soil that had been cultivated no longer sufficed, and a portion of the common mark was taken under cultivation. The chief use of the common mark was in pasturage for the cattle and feeding of pigs on acorns. Besides that, the forest yielded timber and firewood, litter for the animals, berries and mushrooms, whilst the moor, where it existed, yielded turf. The regulations as to pasture, the use of wood, etc., make up the most part of the many mark records written down at various epochs between the thirteenth and the eighteenth centuries, at the time when the old unwritten law of custom began to be contested. The common woodlands that are still met with here and there, are the remnants of these ancient unpartitioned marks. Another relic, at all events in West and South Germany, is the idea, deeply rooted in the popular consciousness, that the forest should be common property, wherein every one may gather flowers, berries, mushrooms, beechnuts and the like, and generally so long as he does no mischief, act and do as he will. But this also Bismarck remedies, and with his famous berry legislation brings down the Western Provinces to the level of the old Prussian squirearchy.

Just as the members of the community originally had equal shares in the soil and equal rights of usage, so they had also an equal share in the legislation, administration and jurisdiction within the mark. At fixed times and, if necessary, more frequently, they met in the open air to discuss the affairs of the mark and to sit in judgment upon breaches of regulations and disputes concerning the mark. It was, only in miniature, the primitive assembly of the German people, which was, originally, nothing other than a great assembly of the mark. Laws were made, but only in rare cases of necessity. Officials were chosen, their conduct in office examined, but chiefly judicial functions were exercised. The president had only to formulate the questions. The judgment was given by the aggregate of the members present.

The unwritten law of the mark was, in primitive times, pretty much the only public law of those German tribes, which had no kings; the old tribal nobility, which disappeared during the conquest of the Roman empire, or soon after, easily fitted itself into this primitive constitution, as easily as all other spontaneous growths of the time, just as the Celtic clan nobility, even as late as the seventeenth century, found its place in the Irish holding of the soil in common. And this unwritten law has struck such deep roots into the whole life of the Germans, that we find traces of it at every step and turn in the historical development of our people. In primitive times, the whole public authority in time of peace was exclusively judicial, and rested in the popular assembly of the hundred, the shire, or of the whole tribe. But this popular tribunal was only the popular tribunal of the mark adapted to cases that did not purely concern the mark, but came within the scope of the public authority. Even when the Frankish kings began to transform the self-governing shires into provinces governed by royal delegates, and thus separated the royal shire courts from the common mark tribunals, in both the judicial function remained vested in the people. It was only when the old democratic freedom had been long undermined, when attendance at the public assemblies and tribunals had become a severe burden upon the impoverished freemen, that Charlemagne, in his shire courts, could introduce judgment by *Schöffen*, lay assessors, appointed by the king's judge, in the place of judgment by the whole popular assembly.* But this did not seriously touch the tribunals of the mark. These, on the contrary, still remained the model even for the feudal tribunals in the Middle Ages. In these, too, the feudal lord only formulated the issues, whilst the vassals themselves found the verdict. The institutions governing a village during the Middle Ages are but those of an independent village mark, and passed into those of a town as soon as the village was transformed into a town, *i.e.*, was fortified with walls and trenches. All later constitutions of cities have grown out of these original town mark regulations. And, finally, from the assembly of the mark were copied the arrangements of the numberless free associations of mediæval times not based upon common holding of the land, and especially those of the free guilds. The rights conferred upon the guild for the exclusive carrying on of a particular trade were dealt with just as if they were rights in a common mark. With the same jealousy, often with precisely the same means in the guilds as in the mark, care was taken that the share of each member in the common benefits and advantages should be equal, or as nearly equal as possible.

All this shows the mark organisation to have possessed an almost wonderful capacity for adaptation to the most different departments of public life and to the most various ends. The same qualities it manifested during the progressive development of agriculture and in the struggle of the peasants with the advance of large landed property. It had arisen with the settlement of the Germans in Germania Magna, that is, at a time when the breeding of cattle was the chief means of livelihood, and when the rudimentary, half-forgotten agriculture which they had brought with them from Asia was only just put into practice again. It held its own all through the Middle Ages in fierce, incessant conflicts with the land-holding nobility. But it

---

* Not to be confused with the *Schöffen* courts after the manner of Bismarck and Leonhardt, in which lawyers and lay assessors combined find verdict and judgment. In the old judicial courts there were no lawyers at all, the presiding judge had no vote at all, and the *Schöffen* or lay assessors gave the verdict independently.

was still such a necessity that wherever the nobles had appropriated the peasants' land, the villages inhabited by these peasants, now turned into serfs, or at best into *coloni* or dependent tenants, were still organised on the lines of the old mark, in spite of the constantly increasing encroachments of the lords of the manor. Farther on we will give an example of this. It adapted itself to the most different forms of holding the cultivated land, so long as only an uncultivated common was still left, and in like manner to the most different rights of property in the common mark, as soon as this ceased to be the free property of the community. It died out when almost the whole of the peasants' lands, both private and common, were stolen by the nobles and the clergy, with the willing help of the princes. But economically obsolete and incapable of continuing as the prevalent social organisation of agriculture it became only when the great advances in farming of the last hundred years made agriculture a science and led to altogether new systems of carrying it on.

The undermining of the mark organisation began soon after the conquest of the Roman empire. As representatives of the nation, the Frankish kings took possession of the immense territories belonging to the people as a whole, especially the forests, in order to squander them away as presents to their courtiers, to their generals, to bishops and abbots. Thus they laid the foundation of the great landed estates, later on, of the nobles and the Church. Long before the time of Charlemagne, the Church had a full third of all the land in France, and it is certain that, during the Middle Ages, this proportion held generally for the whole of Catholic Western Europe.

The constant wars, internal and external, whose regular consequences were confiscations of land, ruined a great number of peasants, so that even during the Merovingian dynasty, there were very many free men owning no land. The incessant wars of Charlemagne broke down the mainstay of the free peasantry. Originally every freeholder owed service, and not only had to equip himself, but also to maintain himself under arms for six months. No wonder that even in Charlemagne's time scarcely one man in five could be actually got to serve. Under the chaotic rule of his successors, the freedom of the peasants went still more rapidly to the dogs. On the one hand, the ravages of the Northmen's invasions, the eternal wars between kings, and feuds between nobles, compelled one free peasant after another to seek the protection of some lord. Upon the other hand, the covetousness of these same lords and of the Church hastened this process; by fraud, by promises, threats, violence, they forced more and more peasants and peasants' land under their yoke. In both cases, the peasants' land was added to the lord's manor, and was, at best, only given back for the use of the peasant in return for tribute and service. Thus the peasant, from a free owner of the land, was turned into a tribute-paying, service-rendering appanage of it, into a serf. This was the case in the western Frankish kingdom, especially west of the Rhine. East of the Rhine, on the other hand, a large number of free peasants still held their own, for the most part scattered, occasionally united in villages entirely composed of freemen. Even here, however, in the tenth, eleventh and twelfth centuries, the overwhelming power of the nobles and the Church was constantly forcing more and more peasants into serfdom.

When a large landowner—clerical or lay—got hold of a peasant's holding, he acquired with it, at the same time, the rights in the mark that appertained to the holding. The new landlords were thus members of the mark and, within the mark, they were, originally, only regarded as on an equality with the other members of it, whether free or serfs, even if these happened to be their own bondsmen. But soon, in spite of the dogged resistance of the peasants, the lords acquired in many places special privileges in the mark, and were often able to make the whole of it subject to their own rule as lords of the manor. Nevertheless the old organization of the mark continued, though now it was presided over and encroached upon by the lord of the manor.

How absolutely necessary at that time the constitution of the mark was for agriculture, even on large estates, is shown in the most striking way by the colonisation of Brandenburg and Silesia by Frisian and Saxon settlers, and by settlers from the Netherlands and the Frankish banks of the Rhine. From the twelfth century, the people were settled in villages on the lands of the lords according to German law, i.e., according to the old mark law, so far as it still held on the manors owned by lords,

Every man had house and homestead; a share in the village fields, determined after the old method by lot, and of the same size for all; and the right of using the woods and pastures, generally in the woods of the lord of the manor, less frequently in a special mark. These rights were hereditary. The fee simple of the land continued in the lord, to whom the colonists owed certain hereditary tributes and services. But these dues were so moderate, that the condition of the peasants was better here than anywhere else in Germany. Hence, they kept quiet when the peasants' war broke out. For this apostasy from their own cause they were sorely chastised.

About the middle of the thirteenth century there was everywhere a decisive change in favour of the peasants. The crusades had prepared the way for it. Many of the lords, when they set out to the East, explicitly set their peasant serfs free. Others were killed or never returned. Hundreds of noble families vanished, whose peasant serfs frequently gained their freedom. Moreover, as the needs of the landlords increased, the command over the payments in kind and services of the peasants became much more important than that over their persons. The serfdom of the earlier Middle Ages, which still had in it much of ancient slavery, gave to the lords rights which lost more and more their value; it gradually vanished, the position of the serfs narrowed itself down to that of simple hereditary tenants. As the method of cultivating the land remained exactly as of old, an increase in the revenues of the lord of the manor was only to be obtained by the breaking up of new ground, the establishing new villages. But this was only possible by a friendly agreement with the colonists, whether they belonged to the estate or were strangers. Hence, in the documents of this time, we meet with a clear determination and a moderate scale of the peasants' dues, and good treatment of the peasants, especially by the spiritual landlords. And lastly, the favourable position of the new colonists reacted again on the condition of their neighbours, the bondmen, so that in all the North of Germany these also, whilst they continued their services to the lords of the manor, received their personal freedom. The Slav and Lithuanian peasants alone were not freed. But this was not to last.

In the fourteenth and fifteenth centuries the towns rose

rapidly, and became rapidly rich. Their artistic handicraft, their luxurious life, throve and flourished, especially in South Germany and on the Rhine. The profusion of the town patricians aroused the envy of the coarsely-fed, coarsely-clothed, roughly-furnished, country lords. But whence to obtain all these fine things? Lying in wait for travelling merchants became more and more dangerous and unprofitable. But to buy them, money was requisite. And that the peasants alone could furnish. Hence, renewed oppression of the peasants, higher tributes, and more corvée; hence renewed and always increasing eagerness to force the free peasants to become bondmen, the bondmen to become serfs, and to turn the common mark land into land belonging to the lord. In this the princes and nobles were helped by the Roman jurists who, with their application of Roman jurisprudence to German conditions, for the most part not understood by them, knew how to produce endless confusion, but yet that sort of confusion by which the lord always won and the peasant always lost. The spiritual lords helped themselves in a more simple way. They forged documents by which the rights of the peasants were curtailed and their duties increased. Against these robberies by the landlords, the peasants, from the end of the fifteenth century frequently rose in isolated insurrections, until, in 1525, the great Peasants' War overflowed Suabia, Bavaria, Franconia, extending into Alsace, the Palatinate, the Rheingau, and Thuringen. The peasants succumbed after hard fighting. From that time dates the renewed predominance of serfdom amongst the German peasants generally. In those places where the fight had raged, all remaining rights of the peasants were now shamelessly trodden under foot, their common land turned into the property of the lord, they themselves into serfs. The North German peasants, being placed in more favourable conditions, had remained quiet; their only reward was that they fell under the same subjection, only more slowly. Serfdom is introduced among the German peasantry from the middle of the sixteenth century in Eastern Prussia, Pomerania, Brandenburg, Silesia, and from the end of that century in Schleswig-Holstein, and henceforth becomes more and more their general condition.

This new act of violence had, however, an economic cause.

From the wars consequent upon the Protestant Reformation, only the German princes had gained greater power. It was now all up with the nobles' favourite trade of highway robbery. If the nobles were not to go to ruin, greater revenues had to be got out of their landed property. But the only way to effect this was to work at least a part of their own estates on their own account, upon the model of the large estates of the princes, and especially of the monasteries. That which had hitherto been the exception now became a necessity. But this new agricultural plan was stopped by the fact that almost everywhere the soil had been given to tribute-paying peasants. As soon as the tributary peasants, whether free men or *coloni*, had been turned into serfs, the noble lords had a free hand. Part of the peasants were, as it is now called in Ireland, evicted, *i.e.*, either hunted away or degraded to the level of cottars, with mere huts and a bit of garden land, whilst the ground belonging to their homestead was made part and parcel of the demesne of the lord, and was cultivated by the new cottars and such peasants as were still left in corvée labour. Not only were many peasants thus actually driven away, but the corvée service of those still left was enhanced considerably, and at an ever increasing rate. The capitalistic period announced itself in the country districts as the period of agricultural industry on a large scale, based upon the corvée labour of serfs.

This transformation took place at first rather slowly. But then came the Thirty Years' War. For a whole generation Germany was overrun in all directions by the most licentious soldiery known to history. Everywhere was burning, plundering, rape and murder. The peasant suffered most where, apart from the great armies, the smaller independent bands, or rather the freebooters, operated uncontrolled, and upon their own account. The devastation and depopulation were beyond all bounds. When peace came, Germany lay on the ground helpless, downtrodden, cut to pieces, bleeding; but, once again, the most pitiable, miserable of all was the peasant.

The land-owing noble was now the only lord in the country districts. The princes, who just at that time were reducing to nothing his political rights in the assemblies of Estates by way of compensation, left him a free hand against the peasants. The last power of resistance on the part of the peasant had been broken by the war. Thus the noble was able to arrange all agrarian conditions in the manner most conducive to the restoration of his ruined finances. Not only were the deserted homesteads of the peasants, without further ado, united with the lord's demesne; the eviction of the peasants was carried on wholesale and systematically. The greater the lord of the manor's demesne, the greater, of course, the corvée required from the peasants. The system of "unlimited corvée" was introduced anew; the noble lord was able to command the peasant, his family, his cattle, to labour for him, as often and as long as he pleased. Serfdom was now general; a free peasant was now as rare as a white crow. And in order that the noble lord might be in a position to nip in the bud the very smallest resistance on the part of the peasants, he received from the princes of the land the right of patrimonial jurisdiction, *i.e.*, he was nominated sole judge in all cases of offence and dispute among the peasants, even if the peasant's dispute was with him, the lord himself, so that the lord was judge in his own case! From that time, the stick and the whip ruled the agricultural districts. The German peasant, like the whole of Germany, had reached his lowest point of degradation. The peasant, like the whole of Germany, had become so powerless that all self-help failed him, and deliverance could only come from without.

And it came. With the French Revolution came for Germany also and for the German peasant the dawn of a better day. No sooner had the armies of the revolution conquered the left bank of the Rhine, than all the old rubbish vanished, as at the stroke of an enchanter's wand—corvée service, rent dues of every kind to the lord, together with the noble lord himself. The peasant of the left bank of the Rhine was now lord of his own holding; moreover, in the Code Civil, drawn up at the time of the revolution and only baffled and botched by Napoleon, he received a code of laws adapted to his new conditions, that he could not only understand, but also carry comfortably in his pocket.

But the peasant on the right bank of the Rhine had still to wait a long time. It is true that in Prussia, after the well-deserved defeat at Jena, some of the most shameful privileges of the nobles were abolished, and the so-called redemption of such peasant's burdens as were still left was made legally possible. But to a great extent and for a long time this was only on paper. In the other German states, still less was done. A second French Revolution, that of 1830, was needed to bring about the "redemption" in Baden and certain other small states bordering upon France. And at the moment when the third French Revolution, in 1848, at last carried Germany along with it, the redemption was far from being completed in Prussia, and in Bavaria had not even begun. After that, it went along more rapidly and unimpeded; the corvée labour of the peasants, who had this time become rebellious on their own account, had lost all value.

And in what did this redemption consist? In this, that the noble lord, on receipt of a certain sum of money or of a piece of land from the peasant, should henceforth recognise the peasant's land, as much or as little as was left to him, as the peasant's property, free of all burdens; though all the land that had at any time belonged to the noble lord was nothing but land stolen from the peasants. Nor was this all. In these arrangements, the government officials charged with carrying them out almost always took the side, naturally, of the lords, with whom they lived and caroused, so that the peasants, even against the letter of the law, were again defrauded right and left.

And thus, thanks to three French revolutions, and to the German one, that has grown out of them, we have once again a free peasantry. But how very inferior is the position of our free peasant of today compared with the free member of the mark of the olden time! His homestead is generally much smaller, and the unpartitioned mark is reduced to a few very small and poor bits of communal forest. But, without the use of the mark, there can be no cattle for the small peasant; without cattle, no manure; without manure, no agriculture. The tax-collector and the officer of the law threatening in the rear of him, whom the peasant of today knows only too well, were people unknown to the old members of the mark. And so was the mortgagee, into whose clutches nowadays one peasant's holding after another falls. And the best of it is that these modern free peasants, whose property is so restricted, and whose wings are so clipped, were created in Germany, where everything happens too late, at a time when scientific agriculture and the newly-invented agricultural machinery make cultivation on a small scale a method of production more and more antiquated, less and less capable of yielding a livelihood. As spinning and weaving by machinery replaced the spinning-wheel and the hand-loom, so these new methods of agricultural production must inevitably replace the cultivation of land in small plots by landed property on a large scale, provided that the time necessary for this be granted.

For already the whole of European agriculture, as carried on at the present time, is threatened by an overpowering rival, *viz.,* the production of corn on a gigantic scale by America. Against this soil, fertile, manured by nature for a long range of years, and to be had for a bagatelle, neither our small peasants, up to their eyes in debt, nor our large landowners, equally deep in debt, can fight. The whole of the European agricultural system is being beaten by American competition. Agriculture, as far as Europe is concerned, will only be possible if carried on upon socialised lines, and for the advantage of society as a whole.

This is the outlook for our peasants. And the restoration of a free peasant class, starved and stunted as it is, has this value—that it has put the peasant in a position, with the aid of his natural comrade, the worker, to help himself, as soon as he once understands *how.*